Dear Ivy,

Just to whet your appetite — thank you for organising such a wonderful day out.

With love,
Diana.

15-8-97.

LUCY BOSTON REMEMBERED

BOOKS BY LUCY BOSTON

Yew Hall
Persephone
Time is Undone (Poems)
Memory in a House*
Perverse and Foolish*
(**reprinted in a single volume as Memories*)

FOR CHILDREN

The Children of Green Knowe
The Chimneys of Green Knowe
The River at Green Knowe
A Stranger at Green Knowe
(awarded the Library Association's Carnegie Medal)
An Enemy at Green Knowe
The Stones of Green Knowe
The Sea Egg
Nothing Said
The Horned Man
The House that Grew
The Castle of Yew
The Fossil Snake
The Guardians of the House

⌘

Lucy Boston Remembered

Reminiscences collected by
Diana Boston

Oldknow Books

Oldknow Books
The Manor,
Hemingford Grey
Huntingdon PE18 9BN

All rights reserved. No part of this publication may be reproduced, stored in a retrieval system or transmitted, in any form or by any means, electronic, mechanical, photocopying, recording or otherwise without permission of the publishers.

Introduction and this edition © Diana Boston 1994
Individual contributions are the copyright of the authors.

ISBN 0-9523233-0-3

A CIP catalogue for this book is available from the British Library

Jacket design by Clare Byatt

Printed in England by
The Lavenham Press
Water street, Lavenham,
Sudbury, Suffolk CO10 9RN

Contributors

Diana Boston	1
Lucy Boston	7
Kenneth Boston	4
Dennis Butts	23
Paul Clough	28
Kenneth East	31
Howard Ferguson	35
James Greene	37
John Guest	39
Diana (Elizabeth) Gunn	44
Peter Gunn	47
Lord Hemingford	62
Annie Rose Hemming	64
Michael Hemming	67
Cally Herbert	69
Polly Hill	73
Peter Hollindale	75
Ian Kellam	80

Frances Linehan	101
Richard Luckett	104
Margaret McElderry	114
Gillian Newbery	118
Philippa Pearce	120
Olivia Rowe	122
Judy Taylor	123
Toby H. Thompson	125
Colin Tilney	130
Elisabeth Vellacott	135
Ann Walshe	136
J.M. Walshe	137
Susan Walshe	140
Nan Youngman	141
Frank Collieson	142
John Rowe Townsend	143
Margaret Clark	146

THE MANOR, HEMINGFORD GREY, Huntingdonshire, is reputedly the oldest continuously inhabited house in the country, built circa 1130. Lucy Boston bought it just before World War II, and restored it as nearly as possible to its original state. She designed and planted a beautiful garden around the house, notable for its topiary, and fine collection of old roses. Later, in her books for children, she recreated the house as 'Green Knowe'. It contains most of her collection of patchworks.

It is now open to the public all the year round, by appointment. Funds raised from the tours of the house, the shop, the books and events held at the house are used for urgent repairs to the house, and for maintenance of the garden. To make an appointment please telephone Diana Boston on 0480 463134.

⌘

to Jill and John, with thanks

Diana Boston

Introduction

Most people who read this book will do so because they either knew Lucy Boston or have come to know her through her books, her patchworks or her ancient Manor House at Hemingford Grey, which she bought in 1937 and recreated as Green Knowe.

For those who might meet her for the first time through this book, I quote what she once wrote about herself:

'I was born in 1892, and even for that faraway date my parents were old-fashioned, so unlikely that I can hardly believe my memories are of real people. The family was rigidly, rabidly puritanical. Music, art, drama, dancing and pleasure were all wicked. My mother thought even good food unnecessary to salvation, and therefore wrong. The most important parental influence over my life was my being specifically taught that I was born and bred to be a martyr, by burning at the stake; it was my destiny and my duty. This I have never felt up to, and have laboured all my life under a sense of absolute spiritual failure.

'We lived in a featureless, new, uninspiring town

full of wealth and churches, and my memories would show a starvation of everything but hymns and sermons, if we had not moved into the country for my mother's health. This was when I was eleven, and from that moment, life was as different as for a butterfly getting out of its chrysalis. I became then like the children in my books: all eyes, ears and finger tips in a world too beautiful to take in. Every moment of day and night was bliss, and had to be prolonged with solitary rambles in the early dawn, of which my elders had certainly no idea. There was no keeping me in, day or night, wet or fine. This is I suppose why my book-children are early rovers.

'We lived in the north, and my sister and I were sent away to boarding school as far south as possible, to correct our north-country accent. We were of course great oddities and were unmercifully ragged and very unhappy. But we learnt to ride and had wild gallops on an old racecourse on the downs. I went to a finishing school in Paris, and thence to Oxford to read English, which I cut short for service in a French hospital in World War I. France became my country of adoption.

'However, I married an English officer in the Flying Corps, as that romantic pioneering body was called. I have one son, the original Tolly — well qualified to draw his own dog, his own toys, his own toy box. I am not a traveller, but have wandered in France, Italy, Austria and Hungary and studied painting in Vienna. I believe that one place closely explored will yield more than continents passed through.

'Now I have found the place I need, and though post-cards from abroad excite me to fever point, this is where I stay, getting deeper in it every moment and always surprised. This is the house that all the books describe. If I were an historian a lifetime could be spent researching into it. But I just sit and talk to it. I live in it alone and find it good company.

'I try to get a book finished in the winter, sitting by Mrs Oldknow's log fire, so that in the summer I can be outside doing the quite vast garden, helped by the dear equivalent of Boggis. My approach to gardening is to find out how the garden would like to be — what wants to grow where. My chief pleasure in it is the interplay of sun and shadow among the trees and on the face of the house.

'My approach to children's books is to write them entirely for my own pleasure at my own age. Perhaps I got stuck at the age of eleven.

'I believe children, even the youngest, love good language, and that they see, feel, understand, and communicate more, not less, than grown-ups. Therefore, I never write down to them, but try to evoke that new, brilliant awareness that is their world'.

There are countless people who have very cherished memories of Lucy. When she died people wrote to us from all over the world. It was brought home to me how very many had been touched and influenced by her life. Some wrote to say that their love and choice of music had been influenced by the concerts she gave in the house during the Second World War. Others were inspired to create their own patchworks after having seen hers. Many planted old roses in their gardens having been introduced to them by Lucy in her garden. Countless complete strangers had been invited in off the towpath, first to share the garden and then to be given a tour of the house which Lucy loved so much. Of course, so many have been and still are entranced by her books. I constantly meet people who loved her books as children and who are now sharing them with their own children.

It is, therefore, more than likely that I have left out people who would have liked to contribute their memories. She kept her life in separate compartments so it was not always easy to track down those who had shared her life. A number of her close friends and her immediate family found it too difficult to write about her so there are obvious gaps. I am very grateful to all those who have contributed — this book is an unedited collection of their reminiscences, written mostly in the first quarter of 1992, the centenary year of Lucy's birth.

I am her daughter-in-law, married to her one son, Peter. She was a splendid mother-in-law; awe-inspiring because of her talents and the amount she achieved in her life. I used to feel that she achieved more in a day at the age of ninety than I achieved at less than half her age. She was an exciting grandmother to our children.

Looking through my mental album of memories I see her sitting at the end of the dining table, the fire blazing, candles lit, patchwork curtains drawn, the family tea (at which there was always a special plate of delicacies for the dogs) over, inventing the most imaginative games with the children. Properly acted charades (in full costume) were her particular pleasure. None of our children would dare to go out on a dark evening to chant the taunting rhyme to Green Noah until they were well into their teens.

Perhaps my most vivid memory of her is in the summer, browned by the sun during the many hours spent gardening until she resembled a piece of beautiful, polished old oak. The birds regarded her as being part of their surroundings and would sit on her head, her feet, her chair, as soon as she stopped to rest. Diana Gunn mentions the blackbird which would wait on the threshold on winter mornings (in summer it flew in and out at will and had the freedom of the whole house). Let in, it would eat bread from Lucy's plate, grapes from the fruit bowl, then would warm itself in front of the electric fire before quietly practising its summer song amongst the feet and chair legs under the table.

But this is not a book written by me; it is time to let Lucy speak, and others recall her in their own words.

⌘

Lucy Boston at her attic window, circa 1977
(photograph Jill Paton Walsh)

Lucy Boston

addressing members of the English Society
at Bulmershe College, Reading,
on 22nd May, 1972

Good evening to you all. I am very pleased to be asked here and I think it's very nice of you all to come and see me. It's always the greatest pleasure for writers to meet some of their public, and I hope a few of you may have read the books when you were at the right age to do so. I hope you are not as shy of me, as I am of you. I don't know at all how you think; how you feel; what you take for granted; what you hope for; or indeed whether you hope at all or despair, and on that point I hope you may tell me later. And besides the gap of two generations that severs most of us, I know nothing at all about Education, for which reason I am now very frightened.

I went to school like anybody else, but must have been quite uneducated, because wherever I go I always find myself less educated than anyone else in the room. So I certainly didn't write my books in any teaching spirit. I see now that I was, in fact, consoling myself.

In my late forties my life was completely dislocated,

as so often happens, and I was looking for somewhere to be and a reason for being there. It's hard to be anything without a milieu to be it in. I had the immense good luck to find a totally compelling house, Green Knowe, no less, on the banks of the Great Ouse. I leapt to it like a pin to a magnet and have been closely held ever since.

In my books for children I invented a family for it with a long pedigree to share its past and its traditions and look forward to its future. I offered the children the idea of a place to which they absolutely belonged. I myself imagined my son living there after me, and his son after that. Of course, now the whole idea of a settled place is nonsense. The past is there, but the future, perhaps, isn't.

Nobody thinks that way any more; more and faster different places is the idea, even though they all get more and more the same. To love a place passionately one must be fairly sure that it exists and has some permanence, and is not a mirage through which a six-lane road will run tomorrow. But not only every loved tree in the complex of hills and valleys, with all their wealth of wild life, may be wiped out for a new town any day; the very planet is now at risk. I think that there is little doubt that the process of destruction will snowball and that we shall understand too late. We shall be sure we shall get what we ask for, but it may not be at all what we expected.

This is the issue of your time; compared with it questions of Protestant versus Catholic, and black versus white, Communist versus Capitalist, are just family quarrels when the house is burning. There is less for you of all the things that make for joy than there was for me, and there will be very much less of all those things for your children. Joy is now a word hardly used, as if people could not imagine what it ever stood for. There is now a new word in common use, 'worsement': a lovely word! The hopeful thing is that this time it is the young generation who are saying they don't like the world that they were born into. The old like me are rich in memories of an earth magical and unexploited, huge, private and to be counted on, to be born in and to die in. I can think of nothing more agonizing to the spirit than to die, for instance, in outer space off orbit. I have adored the natural earth; the words are already hard to put a meaning to.

Only thirty years ago when I found Green Knowe, it was in deep country beside a pastoral river, almost unchanged since my house was built, which was in 1120. My books are therefore very earthy, very rooted, mostly about solitary lost children or an escaped gorilla, who became completely enfolded in a sure place, as real as it is remote, and are passionately and possessively at home in it. And so is every child reader who comes to it: clearly children need it. But in the last twenty years all the country has been whittled away from it. The lanes have become streets; the river flows by concrete banks; traffic roars on the roads all day; and boats looking just like cars follow one another up and down stream, all breathing each other's diesel, while the wake of the boats washes the eggs out of the moorhens' nests.

Development is always the most boring standardization, the obliteration of personal creation and imagination. Pollution is not only of the air and water and the land, and insecticide and weed killers do not only destroy the birds and wild flowers; they shrivel and pollute the mind also. Think of the obvious example, the moon. You probably know the poem:

> Queen, and Huntress, chaste and faire,
> Now the sun is laid to sleep,
> Seated, in thy silver chair,
> State in wonted manner keep ....

How the skies open round it, set to brilliant and spacious music by Benjamin Britten! But nobody will ever feel anything but slight distaste for the moon now; it is merely a mineral globe in our orbit and has litter on it. Or, again think of the oldest joy in the world:

> For lo the winter is past,
> The rains are over and gone.
> The flowers appear again on the earth,
> And the time of the singing of birds is at hand.

'The flowers appear again on the earth', does not mean that on Sunday afternoon all the husbands are bottom-upwards planting out French marigolds in suburban gardens. It means that the whole hillsides and valleys have given birth; hillsides covered with wild daffodils; woods carpeted with lilies-of-the-valley; Devonshire like the milky way with primroses; hayfields more full of flowers than of grass; commons covered with rock roses; banks of wild thyme, hedges of wild roses. I haven't been to Devonshire lately, but all the other places that I've mentioned, that I most love, are now under housing estates. Think what roadsides meant to Thomas Hardy or to Stevenson. If you were asked now by a psychologist to say the first thing that came into your mind after 'roadside', what would you say, 'crash'? Or, litter; charred hedges;

fumes; noise; deadly monotony or just plain hell? Or, consider

> Tiger! Tiger! burning bright
> In the forests of the night,
> What immortal hand or eye
> Could frame thy fearful symmetry?

It doesn't matter that Blake probably had never seen one. When that was written tigers were there by rights, in their own environment, as cruel and as beautiful as the universe itself. It could not be written now, when the tiger has to be protected by acts of parliament or preserved in the vileness of zoos. Anything that's preserved, protected, immediately loses its own natural rights which is its divinity. And whales are vanishing, all the things that most stimulated Man's imagination. 'And there is that Leviathan whom Thou has made to take his pastime therein.'

I wonder if any of you have heard the record of whales singing, that was produced by the Society for the Protection of Whales recently? it absolutely expands your mind to hear it.

Certainly I could never have written *The Sea Egg*, which is my own favourite among my books, if I had known that in the middle of the ocean an area from horizon to horizon is a heaving carpet of our rubbish. It disqualifies the word 'ocean'. At the end of *The Sea Egg* my Triton leaves Cornwall for the Mediterranean, and the word comes in at the close like a benediction. I couldn't think of it without Shelley's 'blue Mediterranean where he lay'. (I won't quote the rest now.) Of course, all classical illusions have dropped out of modern consciousness and they influenced ordinary reading people of my generation more than you could have any idea of, but it is a worsement of consciousness when the Mediterranean can be spoken of as a central sewage basin.

What are we to offer children growing towards such a contaminated future? We cannot offer them pessimism; we should not offer them soft trash. Books, like play, should be practice for life. Easy exercises at first; small children love the ridiculous because it helps to give them confidence. There is a place for the teapot that runs about on legs with an eye on each side of its spout. But what about the six-year-olds? One would not wish to wring their hearts with a story of the death of the last robin on earth. There have been, I know, one or two books about children defending a field or a tree from the developers. But I don't read many children's books and perhaps preservation is now the popular subject. But I wonder as more and more children grow up in tower flats in towns and only see the so-called country from the car window along a motorway, how are we to make them understand what is vanishing? There are the ten-year-olds and upwards who love speed, excitement, danger, space-travel (which are wonderful words) and they're given plenty of it. But how barren space-travel has proved to be. The last journey to the moon was hardly mentioned in *The Times* or on the air, though I believe it was on the 'telly'. But the poor men were out there and in difficulty and we weren't even thinking of them. It's not imaginatively interesting, it requires men trained to be as much like machines as possible. Has poetry been influenced by the cosmic views of the returning astronauts? The vast shining earth hanging over their heads, they must at least have longed to get back to it. It is still our planet, the only place in which we are fitted to live and without which we are nothing.

How can we keep alive the racial memory of this darling, living planet, full of wilful, unmanageable surprise, of unrestricted variety and beauty, shared by millions of other species, akin to us, all actually connected with us — ancestrally connected with us — even the vegetation coming from a common beginning — a teeming richness and mystery, against which we could see ourselves in perspective, and in which we could find our own place?

When I try to imagine writing another book, I simply come up against this: all the words that I would use seem to have lost the meaning they used to have, and I don't know how to go on. Now what about you?

⌘

Kenneth Boston

Almost the last time I saw Lucy, just before her terminal illness, she said to me: 'I think you are the only living person left who remembers me as a girl.' I thought back and supposed that this must be true.

Lucy was my mother's first cousin and was always referred to in our family as Lucy Wood to distinguish her from my mother and one of my sisters who were also called Lucy. She was eleven years older than me and lived, when she was young, in Grove House, Scarisbrick Street, Southport, with her widowed mother Mary (though always known as Aunt James to us), two older sisters and three brothers. Her father, James Wood, had died in 1899, before I was born, but I remember her mother well. She seemed a gentle quiet person and I was fond of her.

Lucy and her brother, and sometimes one or both of her sisters, used to come, it seemed to be nearly every day, to see us at our huge Victorian house called St Wyburn, in Birkdale, about two miles from Grove House, either on bicycles, by walking, or by horse-cab or later, by taxi. One of my earlier memories of her was when I was about four years old. I was walking beside our nurse in Westcliffe Road near our house, beside a pram which contained my younger sister, when Lucy overtook us on her bicycle. She must have been about fifteen, a striking girl with jet black hair, dark penetrating eyes, and an athletic figure. I think she was wearing a school outfit, a sort of gym dress. She stopped and came over to speak to us for a moment. When she had gone I asked Nurse 'was it Lucy or Frances?' In those days to my young mind there was a strong resemblance between the two dark sisters, although I doubt whether Lucy would have liked the comparison.

In the summer, she and her brothers and sisters would come and play tennis with the older members of our family on our grass tennis lawn, and stay for tea in the garden. On Christmas Day, she and others of her family would usually come over to spend the afternoon with us, opening presents round the Christmas tree. As a boy I tended to feel overpowered by her, and I thought her opinion on all matters of art and literature, good taste and general behaviour, to be in a special, ideal category. One Christmas when I was a young boy she bought me a present. I forget now what it was, but I felt very flattered that she had thought of me. I therefore got up from my chair and went across the room to thank her, and to give her a kiss. I was dismayed afterwards to overhear her telling my sister, Anne, that she wished children would not feel bound to give her a 'wet kiss' when she gave them presents. But I also remember on a later Christmas Day her talking to my brother Eric and me about a book of bird sketches he had been given, and pointing out how hard the plumage of the various birds looked in the

Twelfth Night at Grove House, circa 1911. Lucy standing fourth from left; Harold Boston on her left.

illustrations 'as hard as the things they rested on and as the stones beneath. The feathers should look soft,'she said, 'in contrast to the branches and stones.' This remark made a great impression on both of us and made us look at drawings and paintings in a different light.

In those days we spent many winter evenings sitting in the firelight of our drawing room hearth and when Lucy was with us we often took turns to invent or tell fanciful stories; she was particularly good at this game, making up stories that were full of wonder and magic. I remember particularly the beginning of one of these "Far away in the sea there was an island, and on it grew one tree with only one leaf!'

Lucy and her elder brother James (later an artist) had similar interests, especially in literature and the arts, and I think she was greatly influenced by him. In the years just before the 1914-18 war she would come to St Wyburn and spend sessions with my two eldest sisters, Anne and Pat, reading aloud and reciting Shakespeare's plays along with poetry and works by other writers, often sitting in our large conservatory with its flowering plants and their scents. These activities led up to the production by them of two of Shakespeare's plays. Firstly, *Much Ado About Nothing*, which was performed in the large hall in St Wyburn by a cast including Lucy and my sisters, other members of both of our families, and various friends. It was supported by incidental music played by two musical friends on a piano and a cello. Family and friends made up the audience. The second production, *Twelfth Night*, was given in Grove House a year or two later, with incidental music played by Anne (piano) and Spencer Goodfellow (flute), who were also members of the cast. Spencer Goodfellow had been a member of the Hallé Orchestra and his playing was clear, rippling and wonderful to me. I feel sure Lucy was thinking of Spencer's curved lip when, in *The Children of Greene Knowe*, she described Mrs Oldknow telling Tolly to shape his mouth 'into a kind of smile', as he played the flute which they had found in the old toy box.

In about 1910, when she and my sisters Anne and Pat were immersed in Ruskin's views and those of the Pre-Raphaelites, they had the romantic idea of getting up at dawn on May Morning and going into the garden at St Wyburn to bath in the dew on the steep bank that sloped from the middle terrace to the lower one. Whether they ever did this or not I never knew as I was not up so early, and it did not seem to be mentioned any more.

I only saw glimpses of her during the 1914-18 war, but towards the end of it I remember vividly the shock it gave the St Wyburn family when a telegram arrived saying that she and Harold were getting married. The older members of both families were strict Wesleyans, and they looked with anxiety, and often disapproval, at Lucy and her unconventional and often extravagant ideas and actions. They felt that this latest step was too precipitate, and although Lucy and Harold were not blood relations (Harold being the son of my father's first wife, Pattie Lord), they felt it unsuitable, as involving family connections too closely. Of course Lucy was unconventional, daring and impulsive and she tended to be unreasonably biased towards or against people and things in general. But I was surprised when my sister Anne said to me one day: 'under it all Lucy is very affectionate.'

At the end of November 1918, shortly after the armistice, I was stricken by the terrible 1918 flu. I was kept in the school san at the Leys, Cambridge, after all the other boys had gone home for the Christmas holidays and I remember Lucy and Harold coming to see me when I was slowly recovering but still in bed. They brought me some lovely flowers, tulips and daffodils I think, and some oranges wrapped in marvellous rich blue florists paper. It was like a breath of fresh air seeing them both. When I was back at home we had a wire saying Lucy had had a son, Peter, at Kellow Cottage, Looe, Cornwall. They had moved into this quiet cottage on the edge of the cliffs just above the sea and reached by a cliff footpath, the nearest house being some old farm buildings fairly close. Harold called at the Leys at the beginning of the Easter holidays and drove me down to Kellow to see Lucy and Peter and to stay in the nearby farmhouse with Lucy's brother James (Jas) for part of my holidays.

When Lucy and Harold moved to Norton in Cheshire I often used to visit them and stay for short periods. Lucy was very proud of the Georgian house, having furnished and decorated it with great care and hung carefully selected paintings and drawings. On a visit from Norton to St Wyburn at a time when other recently married couples were there she remarked, in the course of a discussion about houses, 'other couples may be awarded better marks on this and that, but I am confident we would be given first prize for our house'.

She was always a devoted and discerning gardener. I used to enjoy going round to various nurseries with her to get special plants that she wanted. In spite of the smoke and chemical pollution from nearby Runcorn and Widnes, she made the garden very beautiful, laying out the lawns and herbacious borders, putting bulbs under trees for spring flowering, introducing small lily ponds and putting a Japanese- type open garden house some way from the main house. This little wooden structure had cane-strip roller blinds on each side which could be lowered to make it a closed room. It contained a divan bed and was used for sleeping out in the garden on warm summer nights but as it was exposed to the early rising sun the rays penetrated between the slats of the blinds and usually awakened the sleeper by throwing piercing shafts of blinding light onto his or her face and boring into the eyes. Hence it became known as 'Gimlet House'.

Lucy was always fond of dogs. The earliest two — Brown, an Irish terrier, and Boaz, a smooth-haired fox terrier — she had in Cornwall, and they came to Norton with her, to be followed by other dogs later. Harold was a keen horseman, and he bought and kept his own horses and got a small pony for Peter, but Lucy, although she rode quite well, was never as keen.

Music played an important part in her life. She and Harold subscribed to the Hallé concerts in Manchester and attended them frequently, often coming back with sharp criticism of the regular conductor, Sir Hamilton Harty, and of performers, especially singers. 'I think he was half tight' said Lucy of Sir Hamilton one night. Handel and the *Messiah* she loved, and she had great admiration for Norman Allin's bass voice in that particular oratorio. She disliked most women singers and could not bear those with trembling vibrato voices but she enjoyed Isobel Baillie's singing, especially in 'I know that my redeemer liveth'. I remember her and Harold coming back after hearing Richard Strauss conduct in Manchester. They were enormously impressed. When I stayed at Norton she would often play us gramophone records in the evening. She was fond of Delius and often used to play 'Brigg Fair' to me.

The music of J.S. Bach was a passion with her. She had records of Harold Samuel's piano playing, of Marcel Dupré playing some of the choral preludes, amongst other Bach music. She once said to me, 'if I am not careful I can get quite foolish about Bach'.

When I was at Cambridge in February 1925 Dr Cyril Rootham presented a wonderful opera production of Handel's *Semele* at the New Theatre. It ran for a week and I invited Lucy and Harold down for it. I remember Lucy being overcome by the marvellous bass aria sung by Somnus: 'When awakened from sleep', 'Leave me, loathsome light', and the following aria 'More sweet is that name'. They were sung by a King's Choral Scholar with a magnificent voice.

I seemed to lose touch with Lucy for some years during the last war but after it ended my wife, Kay, and I used to drive over from Oxfordshire for the day to see her from time to time. Later, Christ's, my old college at Cambridge, began to invite old members to a yearly dinner and night in college. I always tried to call and see her on the way back on Sunday, and stay for a light lunch. She used to call these meetings my 'Geriatric Dinners'.

In her younger days Lucy had intervals when she became devoted, almost obsessively, to a particular subject or activity. When at Norton, ballroom dancing became a passion with her. She took lessons from professional male dancers and attended various Palais de Dances regularly, often taking female friends with her and booking partners for them. About the same time, she became very keen on alpine sports, especially ice-skating, and then her attention switched to lawn tennis. Sometimes these phases would co-exist and then she would gradually lose interest in one or the other.

Lawn tennis was a long lasting interest. She had a hard red tennis court laid down at Norton and then invited various people, mostly girls, to play. Kathleen Carnon (Kay) whom I later married was a promising young player who was being given special coaching by Cheshire County Lawn Tennis Association. Lucy was very fond of her and frequently invited her over to stay at the house and play tennis. Kay had a very individual and graceful way of playing and Lucy, who was good at finding the perfect nickname for people used to call her 'Pony'. Lucy continued to call her by this name until she died.

Lucy could not bear vulgarity and was easily shocked by behaviour which she considered coarse, vulgar or indecent. I remember a time when I was up at Cambridge she and Harold came over for May Week. One day we were slowly punting up the river when, round a bend, we saw a couple in a deep and somewhat suggestive embrace on the bank. I was somewhat surprised to recognise the man as a member of my college. No remark was made at the time by any of us, but when we got back to my rooms Lucy said, in a disgusted tone, 'I did not expect to see that sort of thing at Cambridge. I thought that those who went up to University behaved like gentlemen.' To her, sexual behaviour of any sort should be a private affair between individuals. When I visited her at Hemingford a few years ago she said to me, referring to a pair of dunnocks (hedgesparrows) which I was admiring out of her window, 'They are attractive little birds, but their sexual activity embarasses me.' On one of my last visits to Lucy she said, half jokingly, 'They tell me so many of the Cambridge dons are homosexuals that their race will soon die out!'

⌘

Dennis Butts

A Visitor from Greene Knowe

Lucy Boston had memorable dark eyes which shone out from a face deeply browned from hours spent in her great garden. Her liveliness and the bottle-green trouser suit belied her great age — she was already in her seventy-eighth year when she visited us — and made her seem more like an elvish spirit than the distinguished writer about to address an audience of teachers-in-training in Reading.

I had been introduced to her by Kathleen Lines at the Bodley Head's 70th birthday Tribute to Edward Ardizzone. Naturally I told her how much I enjoyed her writing and how our children were enthusiastic readers, especially of *The Castle of Yew*. Smilingly she took our son's autograph book and wrote for him, 'The Castle of Yew is real and grows in my garden'. It was the first of many kindnesses.

So in 1972, daringly and presumptuously as it seemed at the time, I wrote to ask whether Mrs Boston might be willing to come and talk about her books at the College where I taught. Though professing a complete inability to make a speech "I have nothing to say that isn't already in the books" Mrs Boston did not seem unwilling to appear. 'Especially if I could hear a nightingale, for which Reading used to be famous,' she wrote. She said that she would be willing to meet students and answer their questions.

Undaunted by a threatened railway-strike, Mrs Boston made the journey from Hemingford Grey across London to Reading, arrived punctually, and, despite our efforts to protect her, enthusiastically plunged into a range of activities. (It was as if being cooped up in a railway-carriage had recharged her batteries.) Close-circuit television recording was in its infancy then but she cheerfully agreed to submit herself to a twenty-minute (and very amateurish) interview in an overheated studio before insisting on going out to explore the woods and lake near the Campus in search of nightingales. Over dinner she bubbled about the paper she had decided to give the students instead of simply answering their questions. And she made friends with our children, Tommy (aged 11) and Elinor (10). She gave them a copy of her latest book, *Nothing Said*, signed 'at your house'; Tommy was poorly and in bed that day, terribly disappointed at not being able to meet a favourite writer. But she asked if she could visit him upstairs, and, on learning that he was a keen bird-watcher, questioned him with a mixture of gravity and shy humour, about the kinds of birds he had seen in our garden. (We had a well-loved cat, and she didn't think much of him!)

Lucy Boston's talk was a great success. Delivered in May 1972, it still seems to me a remarkably eloquent address, a prescient and heartfelt plea for our planet but also a moving declaration about Mrs Boston's dilemma as a writer. Question and answers, and some sharp challenges to Mrs Boston's more conservative social attitudes followed, and much, much laughter.

It was simply a splendid visit and when Mrs Boston had negotiated the railway strike and returned home, she wrote (characteristically) to my wife to thank her for 'such restful hospitality', to tell us how much she had enjoyed herself, and to invite us to visit her at the Manor, Hemingford Grey.

A wonderful day followed. With our children and some college friends we picnicked in the garden where much Pimm's No 1 was consumed, poured by Lucy out of a great glass jug, I remember. We were given a conducted tour of the garden, and explored the yew topiary and Ping's hut, and admired the great collection of roses. Many photographs were taken. Then, after tea, we explored the inside of the house, where Elinor was thrilled by the rocking horse and the witch's ball suspended from the ceiling. I remember seeing a copy of Ted Hughes' recent book of poems, *Crow*, on one of the marvellous patchwork quilts in Lucy's bedroom. Lucy Boston, the house, the garden, the river, all seemed quite magical.

We kept in touch with occasional birthday and Christmas cards. In 1974 Tony Watkins and I showed a slide-tape programme about Lucy Boston and her house at the Exeter Conference on children's literature, and she wrote to tell us how impressed a niece attending the Conference, without Lucy's knowledge, had been. 'The family are severe critics as a rule,' she said. When our daughter Elinor sent Lucy a newspaper cutting reporting that the mate of Guy (the model for Hanno in *A Stranger at Green Knowe*) had been removed from London Zoo, Lucy wrote to her 'Poor Guy, I am sorry they have taken his mate away and left him alone again. They are absolutely merciless.' That voice of anger rings down the years.

Sadly our son died in 1976, and it seemed natural that Lucy Boston should be one of the people we should think of at that time. Ever helpful, she invited us to spend our daughter's birthday with her, and tried to lessen our grief. Was it curiosity or some transcendental belief that led her to ask my wife whether she'd seen a ghost of our son? She believed that it was a common experience. Lucy's gentle seriousness under the green shades of the Manor brought some relief.

Lucy Boston was no saint, however. She could be quite waspish at times. Her early books had been published by Faber and Faber, and I asked her once whether she had ever met T.S. Eliot there. 'We passed on the stairs one day,' she said, 'but my editor thought it would not be appropriate to introduce me at that point.' Hearing that she had met E.M. Forster at parties in Cambridge, I asked what he was like. 'I'm glad to see that Virginia Woolf is beginning to get her proper recognition at last,' she replied. Brought up in another era, another world almost, she revealed social attitudes I found unsympathetic at times, but she enjoyed arguing, and enjoyed laughing at herself, too. After I suggested that she was a bit hard on the working classes for wanting the kinds of things she and others had enjoyed for years, she wrote to my wife: 'Tell Dennis I was impressed to hear a workman on the station whistling "Jesu, Joy of Man's Desiring." A wild-looking, filthy man!'

Lucy Boston was intelligent, cultured and perceptive, with some of the assumptions of her generation and background, but with rarer gifts of wisdom and of true originality. Humorous and self-mocking often, she cared deeply about serious things, and, while living a life of remarkable individuality and integrity, wrote with elegance, passion and wit. I cannot help believing that her books and the story of her life with a house will be remembered.

⌘

Paul Clough

It was Lucy's habit in early June each year to invite a group of Cambridge undergraduates to Hemingford Grey to see the house and garden. The roses would be approaching their best and the academic year nearing its end; if the sun shone and the exams had gone well, there were few more delightful ways to spend a couple of hours than meeting so remarkable a person in so special a setting.

And that was how I met Lucy in 1969 — not through her books, or her reputation as a gardener, but at home as a hostess. Considering she knew hardly any of us, as the invitations were always distributed by Jim Ede of Kettle's Yard, she was astonishing in the personal warmth of her welcome and the total lack of reserve with which she shared the house and its contents, the gardens and her intimacy with roses, squirrels and birds. There wasn't the slightest whiff of sentimentality, but there was a considerable air of magic about the almost tangible love she showed for both animals and plants. It was a generous, sharing love, not possessive or exclusive.

When Jim and Helen Ede left Cambridge, it fell to

me to take on the organisation of the annual visit as one of the pleasures of looking after Kettle's Yard. In spite of increasing age, Lucy's welcome for each car load of new faces was as warm as ever. At other times of the year I sometimes had the terrifying job of clipping one of the yew chessmen or some other job that needed a ladder, praying that I wouldn't do it wrong. But even getting it disastrously wrong would have been less frightening than seeing Lucy in her eighties, shears open, leaping to reach the Knight's ears.

During the ten years that I lived in Cambridge, I never read a word of Lucy's books. Looking back, I can't think why; but to read them now with our children is to discover extra layer upon layer about her and her creativity. She welcomed the children as warmly as she had first welcomed those unknown students, treating them as equals from the beginning — just as Mrs Oldknow did with Tolly. Though we only managed to visit her once or twice a year, the friendship grew and deepened to the very last time we met.

Everyone meets a few outstanding people in their lives. I don't expect to meet another with the combinaton of Lucy's gifts. Deeply rooted and spreading her branches wide like the beech tree, she was benign, stable and wise. Her gift for narrative and language makes her books a wonderful pleasure to read aloud or privately. Her eyes could sparkle like a mouse's as she observed the world around. I'm not sad about missing her, because every time I pick up one of her Green Knowe books, she is there.

⌘

Elisabeth Collins

Lucy was an event in my life.

Not a person to be seen around in Cambridge, she would appear from time to time at our door.

Wide, strong, gentle, her eyes flashing, — a concentrated presence.

This is how I remember her. For in her own domain, her house and garden, where we sometimes went, she was integrated — a partaker of, and a giver to, the whole deep magic.

⌘

Kenneth East

Interlude: Great Ouse Run Softly

As the war ended, my squadron migrated from north of the Wash to the softer landscape of the Ouse in Huntingdonshire. Suddenly everyone's thoughts were switched to the prospects of rejoining civilian life. Teachers in uniform were in demand to staff a programme of educational and vocational training. Almost overnight I found myself Station Education Officer. Here was an opportunity to grab resources — office, classrooms, books, periodicals, career pamphlets, etc., and set up a short-lived empire, opening out in as many directions as one could discover.

The unlikeliest of these was the weekly musical evening at Lucy Boston's old manor house in the village of Hemingford Grey. As I bicycled down to the river crossing at Houghton Mill and through the water meadows the darkness suddenly disclosed the amazing dwelling with which later generations of children came to be familiar as the Green Knowe of her books. Coming from our soulless 1940s habitation on the hill, we climbed the magic staircase into a medieval hall, where soft lighting played on romanesque arches, and huge calf-skin covered cushions were spread for reclining airmen as they might have been for returning crusaders. In the midst two handsome sorceresses, Lucy Boston and Elisabeth Vellacott, presided, and Lucy, taking her place beside a gramophone with an enormous horn, announced the first item. In the days of 78 records the pause for changing came every few minutes, with perhaps a word or two of further pronouncement: 'Fugue' or 'Adagio' in her firm tones carried the finality of a command. Somehow one listened to those short segments with a concentration rarely sustained nowadays through LPs and tapes. Her collection of records reflected the purity of taste which was part of her nature, and which she charitably ascribed to us of coarser clay, raising us up in the process. To sustain the metaphor for a moment, she was like bone china among us earthenware. Between my world and hers lay a gap of which I learned to be wary. Asked what instrument I aspired to play I replied the harp — airman's shorthand for the expectation of joining a heavenly rather than an earthly orchestra. Her interest was immediately engaged, and it took some time to detach little by little this false flag from my masthead.

So came about a friendship that took in my children and grandchildren, with visits to that unique garden and house spread over the years. Any attempts to follow her in describing them brings one slap up against Boswell's sense of presumption in writing about 'him who excelled all mankind in writing the lives of others'. What came to me as a shock in her own account — *Memory in a House* — was the tale of suspicion by RAF Security that her hospitality might have a sinister motive and their discouragement of aircrews from attending. All I recall was a stray comment by a colleague years afterwards that it would have been an ideal set-up for such purposes — the inevitable reflex, I suppose, for anyone with the rotten job of policing security. But as I only arrived when hostilities were over, my testimony carries no weight. I knew nothing of past misapprehension. In my book, Lucy and Elisabeth earned medals for our miraculous weekly escape from the drabness of airfield life, with a special ribbon for the true coffee — that almost forgotten beverage — which they magicked from who (that remembers those days) knows where.

Commenting to Lucy on her autobiography, I accused her of using her innocence as a battering ram, and she did not demur. Behind those dark eyes lay an uncompromising certainty of what she was about, what she thought, where she stood. Whatever she touched, whether it was literature, horticulture, topiary, needle-work or simply everyday life, bore the imprint of her unerring sense of beauty and quality. On top of all this was a warmth and a keen sense of the ridiculous wherever it was deserved. On a train journey to London in RAF days I recall her delicious mockery of the self-righteous certainty of the New Statesman I was reading; on one of my last visits her caustic merriment about the self-importance of the TV producers who descended on her for the filming of her creations. Perhaps the purity of her taste at times approached severity; her love of species roses required a merciless proscription of hybrid teas.

The old manor house became a fortress in which timeless values held out against the vulgarisation of our time. Its custodian, lean, wiry and upright in old age, defied the chill of winter within its walls, sufficing, so it seems, with her internal radiation. 'Lucy' I suppose is a variant of 'Lycidas'; our Lucy, unlike Milton's, enjoyed her generous life-span as the genius of her little shore, and was good to all of us who wandered along that delectable river bank.

⌘

Howard Ferguson

Enjoying Music with Lucy

On my arrival in Cambridge my friend Mary Potts, who had been a fellow-student at the Royal College of Music, asked whether I knew Lucy Boston. When I replied 'No', she immediately said, 'We must do something about that.'

As a result, I found myself driving Mary to Hemingford Grey one evening in autumn 1973, being welcomed to the Manor by Lucy, and taking part for the first time in one of those small gatherings that were quite unlike any others I have ever been to. The essential ingredient was always music of some kind: live, of course, and preferably from one of the earlier periods of which Lucy was so fond. Before and after came lively conversation, and to complete the evening there was delicious food and drink.

On this occasion the musicians were the lutenist Anthony Rooley and a small group of singers including Emma Kirkby; but it might equally have been Derek Adlam with one of his own lovely clavichords, or Colin Tilney playing the harpsichord he left at Lucy's for many years.

Whoever the musicians happened to be, the pleasure of listening to them was subtly enhanced by the beauty of the surroundings; for they generally played or sang in the candle-lit upstairs music room, originally part of the Great Hall of the twelfth-century Manor. The one exception was Colin, whose harpsichord refused to go round a bend in the staircase.

Only one of my visits to the Manor was less than wholly delightful musically. Lucy had just been lent a clavichord, and since I was then editing some of the music written for the instrument by Bach's son, Carl Philipp Emanuel, I was invited to come along and play it. Rashly I agreed, quite forgetting that C.P.E. Bach's clavichord had an exceptionally large compass. Inevitably the performance came to an abrupt close when I found myself beating the empty air at each end of the keyboard, in a vain attempt to play the notes that simply did not exist on Lucy's instrument.

No such problems beset the occasions when Lucy came with Elisabeth Vellacott to my house in Barton Road. The evening would begin with a meal in the kitchen, always most flatteringly appreciated. We would then repair to the living-room for what was the real purpose of the visit. I had no harpsichord, alas, but Lucy would kindly overlook that and settle down to enjoy whatever could be offered on a mere Steinway. Generally it was again something that I was supposed to be editing, such as Mozart, Beethoven, Schubert, Schumann or Brahms. Knowing Lucy's tastes, I always suspected she would have much preferred Byrd, Frescobaldi or Bach. But she never gave any inkling of that, and always listened with the sort of rapt attention that makes playing to someone a sheer joy.

※

James Greene

I visited Lucy at Hemingford Grey only twice. I greatly admired her autobiography *Memory in a House* and also, of course, wanted to see the house: its patchwork quilts, its paintings, its garden, the river — nothing could have been more harmonious and Lucy seemed — she was — like someone from a different century, yet utterly present.

In my memory each visit was coloured, and spoilt, by the most terrible rows beforehand with each of the tempestuous girlfriends who accompanied me! So I arrived wrecked and bereft and found myself, ashamed, in the presence of someone whose composure seemed as monumental as the walls; perhaps — far-fetched hope — we could learn from or be reminded by her how to abolish pettiness, how to behave and be! She was in her nineties by then and it was as if everything she said issued from a very deep centre, her own or the house's — who knows? (Perhaps they can't be distinguished.)

On my second visit, in 1987, we brought our daughter Camilla, who was about six months old. Lucy must then have been ninety-five. Conversation was slow because of our uneasy, anguished state of mind — perhaps she was more accustomed to being alone — and she paid more attention to Camilla than to us. We felt happy when she said that meeting her was the best thing that had happened for a long time. (We felt that meeting *her* and the house's eight-hundred-year-old calming atmosphere — amidst our storms — was the best thing that had happened to us for ages). I am left with a memory of a genuine and entirely unpretentious grandeur of an age-old woman who seemed eternally youthful, playing with a very young one; equals despite the gap of nearly a century that divided them.

As if we needed reminding that Lucy could not really be eternal, she asked me to witness her Will. (How many people would let such a thing wait until they were ninety-five?) Thinking to myself 'what amazing trust and confidence to have left it so late', I felt honoured to be asked to play this small part in her death as in her life.

One of the enormous pleasures of parenthood that I can now look forward to is reading Lucy's children's books to our child, as well as showing Camilla, one day, a photograph of herself as a baby with Lucy in the middle distance bending her indomitable looking back as she clips a white rose. To give it to Camilla? We no longer know.

⌘

John Guest

Lucy was my aunt. She had married my mother's brother, Harold Boston, and in those early days they lived at Norton, a village in Cheshire which was only half an hour's drive from our own home. As children, therefore, my brother and I saw quite a lot of her. Norton Lodge was a charming Georgian house situated on a hillside; it looked across a valley of unspoilt country to distant woods. The period was just after the First World War. One of our favourite outings was to be driven by our mother (in our 1923 open two-seater Humber) over to Norton for the day. The house, and the life led there, could not have been more different from our own. Anyone who has read Lucy's autobiography, *Perverse and Foolish*, written astoundingly in her middle eighties, will know that she was — then and for the rest of her life — unlike anyone else. The house and its contents, her appearance, her interests and occupations, were entirely independent of fashion. They were exciting, stimulating, even challenging — and incidentally, heady stuff for the young. I sensed, even then, that my conventional father was inclined to disapprove of these visits, probably on the grounds that they were 'unsettling' for us boys; they might give us a taste for the unconventional, the extravagant; it was surely safer in the long run to be less extreme. Now, with hindsight, it would not have been difficult to see that in Lucy were already the ingredients of a writer, a poet, a talented painter, a fine needlewoman, a notable gardener — one whose essential individuality, as we know from her writing, and especially from her poems, was to lead her always into light or darkness. There were no areas of grey indifference in her life.

Sometimes we went on holiday with her — I remember a time near Looe in Cornwall — when life seemed to be lived at a higher voltage. But the most exciting was a visit to Austria when, characteristically, Lucy suggested that I and my brother and her son Peter should join a gliding school on the Gaisberg, a mountain of green slopes and valleys above Salzburg. It was shortly before the outbreak of the Second World War and many of the young Austrians who were attending the course were already passionately infected with German Nazism. The following brief incident is a digression from the subject of Lucy, but is one that sticks in my mind. I was walking one day with an Austrian who was an ardent Nazi when we got into a political argument. I attempted to counter his convictions and added that, though we might disagree, it was absurd to think that we should actually kill each other for our views. I had assumed our difference of opinion was good natured — but he placed an arm around my shoulder and said quietly, with a smile, 'I would happily kill *you* for *mine*'. At that moment the impending war came suddenly closer.

As a special treat on that holiday Lucy had, with some difficulty and at enormous cost, obtained tickets at the Salzburg Festival Theatre for a perfomance of

Fidelio. Gigli and Lotte Lehmann were the stars, and Toscanini was conducting. I hate to record it but, after a strenuous day's gliding in the mountains, I not only fell asleep during the performance — but noisily so, and had to be woken. The memory shames me to this day as I remember her generosity.

But to return to earlier times, to our visits to Norton. There was always some special excitement, and on this occasion Lucy had obtained a paper fire balloon. It was huge, perhaps six feet long, bright pink, in the form of a pig. In its belly was a wire ring holding a wad of cotton wool which one soaked in methylated spirits and then lit. As the balloon filled with hot air one released it into the sky. We decided to wait until sunset for the launch. It was a perfect evening, a windless blue sky with a full moon. Unfortunately, in unfolding the delicate tissue of the balloon, we found that it was torn in places and had to be quickly repaired. Lucy ran into the house but could find nothing — except postage stamps. Rows of these were extravagantly applied to the pig, and finally all was ready. It was a breathless moment. The huge pig rose steadily into the air and moved slowly away across the darkening countryside. We watched it, spellbound, for ages and ages as it got smaller and smaller, the fire flickering in its belly, until it was a mere pink spark in the distant cloudless blue. This was long before the days of UFOs, and what the astonished locals thought of the phenomenon can only be conjectured. Perhaps with memories of the war they ran for shelter.

Although we did not meet often — Lucy was sometimes abroad and latterly it was difficult for me to get to Hemingford Grey — Lucy was an influence on my life, as she was in the lives of all who knew her. Those who are fortunate to have a copy of her poems, *Time is Undone*, will, by reading them closely, come to understand her better. Despite the appreciation of I.A. Richards of her later sonnets, there is one poem in the collection which seems to me to say, if obliquely, nearly everything she would wish to have remembered of herself. It is called 'Tidal River':

Tidal River

From what withdrawn unsounded main
Beyond the sad drift and the standing pools
Flows back this gull-escorted sea,
   Ebbed waters, for what powers
   The sunken courses do you brim again?

Unfolding floods, your restless mercury
Takes the high clouds and petals them like flowers,
Sways them in ancient rhythm, lulls and flows,
   And in this joining and dissolving rose
   Shows me my hours.

My boat sings interrupted melodies,
Its heedless sides send ripples, far and far,
To those remembered bays, to kiss the strand.

Oh happy ways,
There the belov'd oft-trodden shore,
The cowslip-scented land,
Wait for me still,
Future and past, wait for me still,
   Heart and will
   Exiled no more.

⌘

Diana (Elizabeth) Gunn

Passion — and patchwork. Gypsy — *grand dame*. By some people, far from fools, feared as a witch; she might, in an earlier age, indeed have been burnt as one, enigmatic as was her persona, uncanny her powers; accepted as one of themselves by birds who, with the squirrels, the peacock, the wary pheasant, flocked to her French windows and flew in; or, forming her court as we sat having tea in the garden, perched on her head as they would on the branch of a tree.

And what of the spell she clearly cast on the garden itself? Her ancient yews, their tenure of life, it seemed, renewed with that of the house; the great copper beech, its skirt sweeping the ground in the manner of limes, but surely no other beech; the iris pronounced by her 'eeris', in no way faintly related to the frail, forced, tepid blue of the shop-soiled variety, lustily thrusting four feet high, exotic, tawny as leopards, maroon-cream; in her words 'vinous-smelling, of vanilla and cinnamon'. Do iris, in fact, commonly smell?

With her roses, a tangle of Albas, Damasks, Gallicas, Rugosas, no such question could arise; they could, when she pulled down a bloom to exhibit this, have so seemed to wish to please her, maiden pink, shell-like, striped, purple, releasing each its special scent, demure, spiced, voluptuous; posies of roses stood by the sink in the hall.

A sink! In the Hall? Yes, large, white, ceramic. This too was where the garden entered the house in small, exquisite vases, no Constance Spry effects penetrating to profane the house of which she wrote 'it is a natural thing, made out of the true earth . . . The walls are not heavy . . . They breathe around me'. (Unlike bricks and mortar.) Looking out from the dining room 'you are less in a darkened room than under the actual trees in the lateral but lively light of a wood'. It was by this that the birds were deceived.

Perhaps they were, perhaps it was as simple as this. But what of her own mysterious divination of a Norman house locked within a Georgian strait-jacket, complete with ghosts, heard, and not only by Lucy? When she dispensed with a survey, the vendors enquired 'was she psychic?', a notion at which she must have delightedly chuckled. It was not one in which she would then have indulged, if she later came to do so in the magical Green Knowe books.

My own view of her would be as of the earth earthy and thus closer to the roots of things in a way that has come to seem occult; silent, listening, imbibing the silence of her house in an age when few young people can exist without the beat of tom-toms brought to them by earphones.

Silent even at her own dinner parties, whether communing with the house, enquiring its view of her guests, for the house was a test which you passed or failed to pass. Or simply tired after cooking a perfect English meal, with no frills attached other than excellent wine (if this can be termed a frill), leaving it to her guests to sing for their supper. And, in her seventies, properly so. At no time, though, did she suffer bloomers gladly, the astringent wit of the spoke she would put in when these occurred, crowning the pleasure of such evenings. Possibly her silence provided the acoustics which allowed music to explode in her with the force of a love affair; though she claimed never to understand it.

Lucy, Lucy, how does one put you together? Fastidious, hardy, enduring the bitter winter in a house with no central heating, the great fireplace cold, abstemious, delighting in panache, in Fortnum and Mason to which we owed the down, like no other, of the pillows into which we sank at the Manor. Above all, in late life, as a mistress of the mysteries she evoked for children at Green Knowe, mistress of the written word, must it not be for this that she is remembered? Yes, without a doubt.

Meanwhile so many and so potent are my own memories of her, I am left to pick two at random: firstly her patchwork spread over her knees, threading a needle she could not possibly see, and, as we talked, she in her low voice (a murmur containing a crackle) but with the precision both of articulation and language habitual to her — I never heard her flounder — unobtrusively adding to her magical kaleidoscope. Secondly that of a blackbird, on an arm of her chair, which, she said, daily came 'for a chat' and was certainly 'chatting' to her when we walked in. Disturbed by our interruption of the tête-à-tête, it did not depart but took refuge under the table, where, after remaining silent for a while, it burst into song.

⌘

Peter Gunn

If Lucy in her dedication to *Perverse and Foolish* accuses me of being one of the instigators of the book, I very willingly plead guilty. Her earlier *Memory in a House* had told of the piecemeal revelation of that ancient fabric and the achievement of her enchanted garden, but too little of the lady of the house — how indeed had she achieved that seemingly inscrutable serenity? The span itself of her experience of life, a memory so taut, and a power of expression so robust and felicitous — it simply cried out that she herself give some account of it. Yet I have since wondered how much her memories meant to her in comparison with the intensity of her feeling for the immediacy of the present. With her, memories and the moment must have been very nicely counterpoised, for I have never known anyone more profoundly, silently, immersed in and absorbed by the very fact of her (or his) existence. In Lucy's presence one had a sense that time had quietly withdrawn.

Meeting her late in her life, I was at once impressed by the rugged strength of her face, under the shock of dark hair. The firm mouth, the somewhat fleshy nose, the penetrating quality of very fine wide-set ebony eyes, and, above them, the curves of the pronounced eyebrows, gave her often an expression of quizzical wonderment, an expectant curiosity — and, at times, was it more a hint of melancholy? But the eyes, her eyes were the distinctive feature of her face.

> Two black eyes had little kitty
> Black as a sloe.
> In the garden she used to frolic
> Long time ago.
> (*Nursery rhyme*)

Vide Lucy, aged about three, with her brothers and sisters in the photograph in *Perverse and Foolish*, and that of her alone on a chair, at two and a half, in *Memory in a House*.

Her figure was sturdy but spare; what was immediately remarkable were her hands, large, gnarled and weathered, masculine, like those of a competent artisan. Getting to know her (to the degree that I may be said to have done so), I became aware of the profound depth of her reserve — like that of her house; and what a wealth was immured, retained in that reserve. She gave me the impression that time had tried her severely, and had not found her wanting. To my mind three chief characteristics, each rare in its kind, chiefly distinguished her: her silences (and, not unrelated to these, her simplicity, the simplicity nevertheless of a *grand dame*; then, her extreme fastidiousness, an exquisite refinement both sensuous and moral; and, thirdly, her uncanny affinity with animals and birds. In pondering her possession of these attributes, themselves rather unique, but stranger still as cohering in one person, it has occurred to me that perhaps their coincidence was not altogether fortuitous, that they may have had some linked or common origin. In *Memory in a House* and *Perverse and Foolish* she has (at least it seems to me) gone some way to point out to us from whence these qualities derived.

Nothing can be more gratuitously presumptuous in some contemporary biographies than psychological analyses (Freudian or otherwise) that claim to reveal hidden parental, infantile or adolescent occurrences in the subject's life that are alleged to account for subsequent behaviour. Nevertheless it would be unwise to ignore such evidence when it exists. Lucy, writing *Perverse and Foolish* at the age of eighty-six, is explicit enough, recalling certain events of her youth with a vividness that reflects the importance she attached to them. At the risk of appearing *simpliste*, I am suggesting that these remarkable facets of her character owe much to the occurrence of a most severe mental and moral ('spiritual' is the most fitting word) trial, which she underwent at a most impressionable stage of her life. The outcome of this crucial inner conflict was Lucy's complete mastery over herself: the fullest, most passionate youthful play of all her youthful senses was triumphantly held in check, brought under an inflexible control, by a prolonged exercise of a scrupulous honesty and an immaculate chastity. I write 'triumphantly', and, I think, with reason; but Lucy may appear to have questioned the triumph. In her little book of poems, *Time is Undone*, published privately in 1977, when she was eighty-five, the poem 'The Immaculate Refusal' suggests some second thoughts:

> Against his breast, with a fool's faithful No
> I let bright heaven and all creation go, . . .
> So that the days disoriented fly
> From unconsenting mortals such as I.

Her mother was the very antithesis of Lucy, their natures entirely dissimilar. While Lucy, inheriting much of her father's verve and energy, was vitally active, eager for 'the bombardment of new sensations and the emotional vistas of mere living' (*Perverse and Foolish*, p.95), her widowed Mother was retiring, 'gentle and nervous', morbidly aware of the dangers of sex — she engaged in Wesleyan 'rescue work' among the 'fallen' young women at Southport workhouse. As young girls, her sister Frances, two years her senior and her mother's favourite, was innocently flirtatious, while Lucy was *noli-me-tangere* virginal. Nevertheless in her teens she became aware that her mother was watching her 'with growing concern', as 'something she neither understood nor trusted' (*Perverse and Foolish*, p.59). In the summer before she went up to Somerville, just after the outbreak of the First World War in 1914, the family were staying at the house they rented annually at Arnside in Westmorland. With them were their Wood and Boston cousins. Lucy was in her twenty-second year. It was this summer, she relates in *Perverse and Foolish*, that her 'gentle and nervous mother became Public Enemy No. 1.' Her cousin Wilfred Wood was not regarded as good-looking, but he was charming, a well-informed, cultivated young doctor, who liked going on long walks in exploration of the beauties of the countryside. Lively and engaging, he was everyone's favourite; all the girls loved him. As the most active of the family, Lucy usually accompanied him on his walks. One hot day, resting after a climb to overlook Windermere, he lay with his head on her lap. At home, pleased by this singular mark of what she deemed an honour, she confided in her elder sister

Mary that she thought this natural gesture of Wilfred's showed that he must like her. Mary informed her mother. Next day an embarrassed Wilfred told her that they had been forbidden to walk alone together. Worse was to follow. The summer was excessively hot, and the young had taken to sleeping out of doors on the lawn. It was there, lying with the others on adjoining pallets and looking up at the heavens overhead, that Wilfred pointed out and named to a most interested Lucy the constellations and individual stars. Their conversation, whispered so as not to disturb the sleepers, was watched from a bedroom window by her troubled Mother. The following morning she was told not to sleep next to Wilfred again; she must lie as far away as the restricted garden permitted, or else indoors. Years later Lucy recalled the force of her indignation: 'Disgust and contempt were my reactions. Did innocence not exist for her? My rejection of the insult was violent enough to set me on a course of outrageous and defiant unconventiality whenever the opportunity offered.' Increasingly it was in the company of her three older brothers that she found that she 'shared a world of candour, trust and decency' — they had 'no fear for each other's behaviour'.

To her mother's fears were now added her utter dismay, when the time came for Lucy to be received into the Wesleyan community. Despite regular private sessions with the minister and her mother's tearful pleadings, she refused. Lucy had, and always retained, a peculiarly religious cast of mind, and she has expressed the trepidation and regret that she felt in abandoning the faith of her fathers. For her, entire honesty was an unassailably ultimate touchstone in all matters.

The lack of trust shown in her by her mother seems to have acted on her as both a sanction and a challenge. If her mistrust was justified, Lucy's own conscience would provide the sanction. The challenge she herself had set, and accepted. It was a perilous challenge. It might be said that the qualities she now evinced in this protracted test were qualities she already possessed, as innate, or rather as reflecting the best in the evangelical ethos in which she was brought up. This could have been so; yet other young women, in similar circumstances, might have acted differently. That her innocence was suspected brought out fierce qualities of resistance.

There were profound elements in Lucy's character which the trauma of her mother's distrust of her served only to strengthen; it encouraged her already formidable will-power. If her personal behaviour was even so much as to be indirectly questioned, she had at her command a healthy confidence in herself, in her own powers of judgement, which developed in time into something like a stoical independence. It would seem as if she early made an internal vow that in her relations with men she would offer and receive such gifts of friendship that were seemly in her sight, and if this did not include sexuality, then she preferred to remain virginal. It seemed that she aimed at an ideal of passionate chastity. All her life she was to have a horror of any form of promiscuity. The calls of senses so vibrant and subtle as hers required of her a stance that was one of eager reticence, a fervid reserve — a balance not easily achieved.

As a very attractive young woman, in appearance as well as intelligence, her presence was much sought after by young men, both among her relatives and their friends at home and others in wartime France when she worked as a V.A.D. at the French military hospital in Normandy. The morals at the hospital were lax; the French night nurses were found in the morning in bed with the wounded *poilus*, and were dismissed. The English V.A.D.s seemed to have been the mainstay of the establishment. An upper-class young Frenchman, serving as an anaesthetist, fell in love with her, proposed, was politely declined, but remained a firm friend, Lucy visiting his parents in Paris and his uncle's shooting lodge deep in the Normandy countryside. This young man, when asked by others in the hospital, 'Was there anything going with Miss?' replied, 'Try it. You will see.' Lucy commented, 'He had more faith in me than my mother.' If she was asked if she would like to go for a walk in the evening, she might agree, and accept the offer quite literally. She would take her admirer on a spanking non-stop English walk of some ten miles — and leave with cordial thanks for a pleasant evening. How deeply her mother's distrust of her relations with men had wounded her is seen by other remarks in *Perverse and Foolish*: 'For the would-be amorous man I had a laughing but friendly contempt. There was no malice in my behaviour nor any aggressive ideas of Women's Lib. I thought I was proving my mother wrong again.'

However, there were two sides to the coin — this coin of the city whose tutelary was Artemis. In England before the War Lucy had seen much of Harold Boston, who was something of a relative — his stepmother was a Wood cousin, who had married on his first wife's death a Boston of Southport. In the summer of the outbreak of war Harold was staying with the Wood family at Arnside, where he, the boys and Lucy spent much of the time in a spirit of male camaraderie trying out their newly purchased motorbikes. Later, when her three brothers were up at Cambridge, she joined them, to do part of her V.A.D. training at Addenbrooke's, and lived with Jas at his lodgings on King's Parade, where they were visited by Harold, who was at an officers' training camp nearby. So close and matter-of-fact was the relationship among the young that one night, when Harold was with them in King's Parade, Lucy, having had an hallucination that he was present in her bedroom, went up to his room, and finding him there, slipped into bed beside him, 'as naturally as she would have joined him in a punt'. They lay, the length of their bodies touching, but it went no further. That summer she took to sleeping out in a punt by Byron's Pool, where Harold would join her for an hour or two from camp. One morning, waking alone, she found a kingfisher had alighted on her wrist. She rightly saw it as a portent.

When, in 1916, she received her embarkation order for France, she spent the last evening in London with Harold, who was recovering from a serious motorbike accident. Missing her train, Harold accompanied her by taxi to Southampton. On the way he first kissed her. Later, home on leave, they spent an enforced night together at the George Hotel in Huntingdon, where, Lucy informs us, their 'well-mannered intimacy was screwed up a turn tighter.' At home or in France, where Harold was serving, they spent their leaves together, sharing rooms and bed, but abstaining from love-making. Perhaps the height of this extraordinary platonic relationship, so bizarre to our contemporary *mores*, was reached, when they stayed in the gilded Edwardian luxury of the Hotel Crillon in Paris in a bedroom described by Lucy as fit for a Ninon de Valois. This was passionate chastity indeed, and it could hardly be sustained. In *Time is Undone* she looked back, recalling how she arrived at a decision:

> I saw my heart's desire lie close to me
> Saying Try me, try me and see,
> Receive me all, let love made perfect now
> Absolve you from your vow.

Lucy married Harold Boston in 1917.

Of her nearly twenty years of marriage apparently she seldom spoke — to me never, except to express the terror she experienced at the speed with which her husband drove his very fast cars — Bentleys. (Later in life, she preferred a leisurely twenty-five miles an hour.) In *Perverse and Foolish*, with her characteristic honesty, she questions the wisdom of her 'immaculate refusal', with its consequences unforeseen at the time; and in *Time is Undone* she sounds a note which suggests that of a measured regret — 'a world of bliss' set against 'the terror of the outcast years'.

After the dissolution of her marriage, Lucy spent some years in Italy and Austria painting — 'with passion' she confides, but she had no need to do so, since everything she ever did was done with passion. Mussolini and Hitler between them cut this short. Back in England, in 1937, and installed in lodgings next door to those she had previously shared with her brother Jas, opposite King's, where her son Peter was now in residence, she heard one day quite casually that there was a house up for sale at Hemingford Grey. In her mind's eye she saw a house that she had first seen from a punt on the river in 1915, and had unknowingly fallen in love with. She bought it; and so began Lucy's second great love affair. The Manor House at Hemingford Grey fulfilled exactly her ideal of a love of passionate chastity.

To see Lucy as the châtelaine of her Norman house in the setting of its ordered wild garden was to see how perfectly she was to fulfil the role. There she gently took possession of the silence, directed all things in accordance with her fastidious taste, and delighted in her closeness to living nature, to the landscape, the river, the garden and all its small inmates. In that prolonged struggle to establish, or to confirm, her womanly integrity, where actions counted most, what need had there been for words? — she had learned that silence was best. And she found now this silence echoed in the house; it spoke to her in silence. Silence, reticence, simplicity, reserve — with the years they had become second nature to her. In *Memory in a House* she accuses the present generation of having no conception of silence (or do they perhaps agree with Berlioz that its effect can be best achieved by ten massed military bands?) The silence that she alludes to is that of 'abounding life', an enveloping stillness, which you 'broke into' and it 'closed round' you again. The discovery of a new domiciliary silence, as the restoration of the manor house progressed, fascinated Lucy. She found 'that one of the qualities of the Norman hall became its strength and most inescapable feature. It has a pronounced, contained and powerful silence that is a continuing challenge.' It is as if the beautiful light-coloured stone-work of the massive Norman walls breathed in sound and transmitted it into a quite audible silence — but not to 'the sensual ear'. In her dining room I have seen Lucy sit listening, attentive to the whispered silence of the surrounding walls. For her the house was animate, infused with its own pulsing life. She had carved on its principal tie-beam the words *Vocatus atque non vocatus deus adest*. ('Whether invoked or not, there is a god present.') So much was she susceptible to the 'divine' silence that it seemed to her that even to transpose one's experienced impressions or thought into words was something of a profanation — she confessed that she never could see hoar frost again with 'surprised rapture' since she had put it into words in *Yew Hall*. Music, heard in this house, affected her deeply; she felt that the house was 'built by music, permeated through and through by it, held in place by it'. Being once surprised by the realisation that she was hearing it *now*, she admitted that 'the present is a tense that I am seldom aware of'. She could have meant by this that she was more acutely aware of the internal (silent) experience produced by her outward senses than of the moment at which it occurred. So open and alert were all her senses that her reception, her acceptance, of the world might be looked on as essentially aesthetic — and I think that even moral concerns affected her in this way; she lived, as it were, in a continuum of heightened feeling.

To those who did not know her well her own silences could be disconcerting; and not the less so, when broken by one of her more astringent observations. Silence would follow her from the house to the garden. There, for hours working in close association with her gardener, she would mutely dig, weed and plant, each of them immersed in her, or his, own thoughts. It is but natural, therefore, that in her poems silence should find so prominent a place:

> Silence has mastered all our joys.
> In it alone our thoughts can take
> Their movement and their poise.

And she can recommend, from the depth of her own experience, the Roman augurs' *Favete Linguis*. (Be silent that you may hear.)

Lucy's fastidiousness, her taste, applied in all she did: in the decoration of the house, the silver and the handmade china that she daily used — even the willow-wood she grew, cut and burned on her fire; in the lay-out of the garden and the choice of plants (especially the roses); in the music she continually listened to, and the painting she once practised and always enjoyed; in the books she read, and above all in those she wrote; in the conversation which, if often silent herself, she encouraged ... This taste of hers was epitomised, or perhaps highlighted, in the delightful — however sybaritic it may appear in contemporary eyes — gatherings she would hold on a still summer evening in the coolness of the garden, when we drank champagne or a good hock from the petalled cups of personally chosen specimens from her old-fashioned roses — from Hebe's Lips herself. The scent of the flower, adding a delicate bouquet to the wine in a way that Gluck would have approved, gave a pleasure that was quite exquisite. For Lucy a scentless rose was no rose at all — scent always presented her with an insoluble mystery, as being 'the most immediate of the senses, seeming to reach straight into the unconscious, unanalysable and profoundly moving. It can produce the same kind of awed delight as great art ....' It does not seem to me too far-fetched to see the extreme refinement of Lucy's reactions to the scents of flowers, to art, literature and music, and to discriminating friendship — a refinement combined as it was with the fastidiousness of her daily living and her sensitivity to moral issues — as the outcome of her earlier spiritual conflict: her intrepid confrontation of the imperious impulses of her passionate awareness of being with a rectitude that was her own, her highly personal interpretation of her evangelical upbringing. However dearly the victory cost her, she won through to the seeming serenity, marked perhaps by that underlying melancholy, of the woman, so versatile and fascinating, that we all knew and whom to know was to respect and to love.

It may appear a tenuous link that could join this critical period of her adolescence and young womanhood with the extraordinary affinity Lucy showed with the small creatures of woodland and garden. In the countryside animals will continue their activities quite gregariously, undisturbed by the presence of others of a different kind — horses, cows, sheep, deer will pursue their grazing, indifferent to each other or to the comings and goings of rabbits, squirrels and birds. I have seen a finch alight on the back of a cow, who placidly went on ruminating, impervious to any intrusion. If certain creatures have particular enemies in other creatures, it is man whom they all eye askance. Lucy was singular in that the animal world seemed to have made her an honourary member of its own league. While she sat having tea in her garden, tits, finches, robins and sparrows would perch on her shoulder, pick crumbs from her plate, rest on her teacup. The squirrels would gently rap on the glass of the French windows of the dining room, and when opened, enter, aware of the great bag of peanuts around the corner. They might be joined in this daily distribution of Lucy's largesse by wood pigeons, blackbirds, thrushes, pheasants — even, I believe, on an occasion by a deer, or was it a peacock? Once, we arrived to find Lucy sitting in front of the fire in her Elizabethan fireplace and entertaining a blackbird, who nonchalantly, as if quite at home, proceeded from under the dining-table to perch on her chair, and there to give the opening bars of his song. One remembers the kingfisher that alighted on her wrist as she slept in the punt at Byron's Pool, and wonders whether that stillness that served her then was a reason why birds in her presence always showed such a pronounced forbearance. But it was not simply their tolerance of her — she seemed positively to attract them. It may be the profound reserve that she had developed, when she set herself the challenge — her silences and stillness, suggesting a welcome in her reticence — had much to do with this uncanny gift of hers. But to call it 'uncanny' is to admit it genuinely inexplicable — real, but quite mysterious.

Notwithstanding all that Lucy wrote about the spirit of the house and the enchantment of the garden, it was she who was the true *genius loci*. If the Normans built the house, she recreated it, resuscitating its ancient stones with a new breath of life. And she herself created the garden. This idyllic setting saw the birth of her books. In it, at the advanced age of sixty-two, she wrote *Yew Hall* where perhaps the principal character of the novel is the house itself. Then followed the splendid series of the *Green Knowe* books for children, considered classics in her lifetime, where again house, garden, river and countryside are evolved at different historical periods — her last gift to intelligent children. There at Hemingford Grey she spent long days working in the garden, listening to music in the evenings, entertaining her friends, and increasingly showing round visitors. Everything she did was a labour of love. And, as we may read in the last poems in *Time is Undone*, love came to Lucy again in her old age with as clear a call as ever, a love which as it unfolded itself revealed once more that unique quality which had characterised her two earlier great loves — her passionate chastity. She herself has expressed:

> How slight a chance brings on our destiny!
> If death had come when it was due
> I should have died as one who never knew,
> Without this great content to go with me.

⌘

Lord Hemingford

A great watershed in my family's relationship with Lucy was when — it must have been in her late 70s — she finally consented to be given a lift home when she came to lunch. Until that time she had insisted on walking both ways between the Manor House, Hemingford Grey, and the Old Rectory, Hemingford Abbots — a distance of about one-and-a-half miles.

Lucy probably would have had more excuse for pretention than most people we knew but she was in fact utterly unpretentious. Indeed I have known few people more straightforward. She always said what she thought and if it was less than enthusiastic she managed to convey it in such a way as to suggest it was, after all, only a matter of opinion and, while she held passionately to her view, she was not surprised if others did the same. I do not think it would have been possible to have an argument, as distinct from a difference of opinion, with Lucy.

For example, I often used to tell her that there was much on television which she would enjoy. She was monumentally unpersuaded. In fact she refused to listen to the argument. In most other people this would have been infuriating, but Lucy's conviction was so amiable that I usually ended up feeling that it was I who was being unreasonable.

Her other most notable characteristic was her interest in the young. Most people's enquiries about one's children are polite and perfunctory. Lucy actually wanted to know and — unsurprisingly from the author of *Perverse and Foolish* — the more unexpected the stories were, the more delighted she was and the more bubbly that distinctive giggle would become.

She and my mother shared much, including a love of roses and an ability to appear at first sight formidable. My father shared her love of words; my wife her warmth of personality. My children were variously addicted to Green Knowe and to feeding the squirrels with chocolate-covered peanuts. No wonder I miss her.

⌘

Annie Rose Hemming

I was told that the first time I met Lucy was when she was having tea with my mother at our house in Budapest, about 1936 or 1937. I was then 16 or 17 years old and at school. Strangely I have no recollection of the event, which ultimately was to change the course of my life. My mother approached Lucy in 1938 to ask whether she happened to know of a family with whom I could 'au-pair' for a few months, to practice and improve my then basic English.

It was then that I found myself staying with Lucy at 15 Kings Parade, Cambridge, at the end of October 1938, feeling very strange and shy. I marvel still at Lucy's kindness and generosity. At the time she had a young Austrian refugee on his way to the United States, staying with her, and as well she was trying to rescue a Jewish family still in Germany by paying for their release — alas without success.

For me there followed the most wonderful and formative period of my life — months that I look back to with nostalgia when the going is rough.

Lucy opened windows for me: the Cambridge colleges, Evensong in King's College Chapel, St John's Passion by candlelight, the Carol Service at Christmas (which we would not miss for the world on the radio on Christmas Eve, even now) and the Beethoven Quartets played by the Pro Arte Quartet at the Arts Theatre, as well as Lucy's huge collection of records. Artists and musicians visited and I heard much to interest and inform me.

I was taken to see London, and some of its museums, and to a performance of *Hamlet* in modern dress (was it John Gielgud?) When we came out of the theatre London was wrapped in thick fog and we had missed the last train. A taxi was found to take us back to Cambridge. I think it took four hours and at one point we seemed to be in a field.

We went to the Cambridge Arts Ball, for which costumes were hired. Lucy looked sumptuous in a purple crinoline and won a bottle of champagne as the Belle of the Ball.

I was staying with Lucy some months later when she was told that a house was for sale in Hemingford. She immediately wanted to go and view it. I remember the astonished face of the owner at the door: 'Yes, it is for sale but we have only just decided to sell and we have not even advertised it yet!'

It may have been another house that was advertised but it was not untypical of Lucy; there were other accounts of second sight.

Lucy without fail always stood by me at critical times in my youth. During four months of internment she sent me a large box of Tiptree jam, almost unobtainable, and during a rather lengthy illness not a week passed without a delivery of a large box containing an assortment of wonderful fruit — again at a time when it seemed unobtainable in shops.

Again, when clothes rationing was at its most severe, she sent me six yards of luxurious cream silk for my wedding dress.

What a wonderful friend she was to me and how privileged I feel to have known her!

⌘

Michael Hemming

Lucy was in a way a second mother to me. I think my first contact with her was in 1919 soon after my birth, an occasion that I do not remember but ever since then I have intermittent memories of her throughout my life. She was strikingly beautiful with flashing and piercing brown eyes which seemed to pierce into one's inmost soul. I remember her as the first naked woman I ever saw.

In early years I used to stay with Aunt Lucy, Uncle Harold (Uncle Thrash) and my cousin Peter. At night we would settle down in our dormitory containing Peter, me and my brother John. Uncle Thrash would come in with a papier-mâché wolf mask on his head to frighten us. Lucy would read us exciting stories from *The Master of Mysteries* and other books. Sometimes there would be wonderful stories which she invented as she went along. She never lacked imagination.

My memories of her at that time are of a strong mistress of a household with housemaid, cook and gardener. She was surrounded by dogs: Murphy, a bumbling senior citizen of an Airdale, Jake, a powerful young Alsation on whose back I tried to ride upstairs and Charlie, a greatly loved playfellow fox terrier.

The house stood in a beautiful garden with lawns, a Japanese summer house, a pond full of frogs and beyond, a vegetable garden. A field for the horses stretched below the ha-ha down to a canal and railway, both sources of interest for young boys. There was a tennis court and an interesting yard with stables at the back. The house as I first knew it was lit by oil lamps and candles. There were rumours of ghosts enhanced by 'The Death Bed', a large bed, canopied in white, next door to some noisy plumbing.

I associate Lucy with very good holidays. She took us to Looe on a number of occasions to stay in a cottage above Plaidy beach and in my teens to a farm near Gunwalloe. Later we went to Austria for a skiing holiday at St Anton. Lucy collected some attractive young girls round her, one of which I married. I made frequent visits to Cambridge and later, sporadically through our lives, to Hemingford Grey, until we said farewell to her just before she died.

⌘

Cally Herbert

My childhood memories of the Manor House are ones which I feel must have originated from the stories Lucy told me and my siblings about the house and its other residents, fuelled by a rather lively and ridiculously melodramatic imagination.

On visits to my grandparents, who lived in the neighbouring village, it was a great treat to walk with my grandmother along the towpath between the two villages on a visit to Lucy. To keep us amused there were many things along the way which my grandmother used to show us every time. These included windmills, wild flowers and, in particular, a notice by a wall which seemed to contain overgrown chaos. It stated it was advisable to keep out due to the presence of poisonous snakes. This was on the part of the path leading past Lucy's home and was the first indication of something unusual behind the wall. The same question was always asked, 'Are there really snakes in Lucy's garden?' As we rounded the bend Lucy would always be there, either standing at her gate chatting to passers-by or hard at work tending her garden. There was the house too; the coronation pieces standing to attention along the path leading to the front door of a house which seemed to have seen so much happen and still to be watching with its huge rectangular eyes. You could never see in through the first floor 'eyes'. It felt as if you might see someone from a different era if you were able to peer inside. Lucy would greet us with a cheery smile and a warm-hearted giggle and walk with us up to the front door. The plaque of a fierce dog declaring CAVE CANEM was enough of a warning to any small child that something unusual might happen. The mirror at the far end of the entrance hall, the birds' nests lining the walls, the huge witch's ball in the front room, the eneven floor, the dark dining room with its ageing photos of Guy the Gorilla and the picture made from human hair over the fireplace (up which you could see the sky), the squirrels and birds coming to the French window to feed on nuts from Lucy's hand, the overpowering beech outside the room, all served to enliven my imagination.

I can vividly remember feeling extremely apprehensive about entering the dining room on my own and would silently rehearse words that I would say to any previous resident I found there. I imagined Lucy sitting there alone conversing quite happily with them and sometimes I almost wished that I could be there too.

It wasn't until I spent two days a week helping Lucy with her cleaning that I really felt more at ease in her home on my own. One day I spent a whole morning cleaning and polishing the entrance hall floor and afterwards I felt that I knew every stone and all the feet that had tramped over them. Another day my morning was spent in her bedroom, the upstairs room with the 'eyes'. It was summer with the accompanying outside noises. I heard a child laugh and immediately my senses pricked. I was sure that if I looked out of the window I would see Tolly playing in the garden. The music room next door gave me just as powerful a sense of its past, something seemed to be keeping a watch on me so that I didn't leave anything out of place to disturb its peace. However, a visit up the stairs from here to the attic room on my own was still out of the question, despite the lure of the Squeaky Doll and the Rocking Horse (childhood favourites). Lucy's description of the blocked-up room was still too vivid in my mind. As I grew to know the house as only someone who cleans a house does, my apprehensions about being in the house diminished. I felt very low to think that Lucy's home might have to be sold after her death and she would have to see it change. It is a unique house which belonged to a unique and very special lady.

Having re-read all the Green Knowe books for a dissertation and talked to Lucy about her life, I began to realise that this was not an old lady who simply wrote wonderful stories and created beautiful patchwork quilts, but someone who had lived her life to the full in her own individual way. Her religious Lancashire upbringing, the driving of an ambulance during the Great War, the marriage to her cousin, her adventures in uncovering the house and the musical evenings she gave to servicemen during the Second World War made me admire and respect the rich variety of her life. She appeared to be an excellent role model for any modern supporter of feminist ideals. Lucy rarely talked to me about her early experiences; with her unassuming manner she may not have seen the significance her life had for me and my siblings. Her life seems to have been full of daring originality but I don't imagine it was ever planned to be like that.

I have a romantic image that her life was free from thoughts of money, insurance, mortgages and all those other avaricious tendencies that seem to be so important in our lives these days. I envy the opportunities Lucy, as a woman, was given in a time when individuality and non-conformity were a ticket to adventure, rather than disapproval.

I feel very sad that any children I have will never know Lucy and experience the richness of her life.

⌘

Polly Hill

Time is Undone

(All quotations are from L.M.B.'s collection of poems *Time is Undone*, 1977.)

O canopy of age, of creeping years,
beside the Ouse the waters rise and play,
no cause for weeping in manorial stones
but celebrate the order of the day!

Our Ouse rose high and blanked memorial plains
Viz water meadows fat with purple cows.
The waters pass our lovely Lucy by
her thick-walled castle low but very dry.

O celebrate, we said, since eighty-seven
is but three times the prime of twenty-nine.
"Unfolding floods, your restless mercury"
assert the level of this special time.

Time is undone and overdone and torn,
time is an error which we must ignore.
The steepled landscape, now not Hunts but Cambs,
"Takes the high clouds and petals them" be-

fore.

O Lucy wise beyond your years and ours,
permit this celebration in bad verse.
Our love concealed may yet just percolate
"Out of long lineage, bearing still your face."

        10th December, 1979

Peter Hollindale

Given at the Memorial Service, October 13, 1990

When a long life comes to an end, and the life is that of a much-loved person and a much-loved writer, and people gather as we have this afternoon to express gratefulness for the life which is over, there are really two congregations here to commemorate it. One, and in truth the more important one, is that of the people who knew Lucy Boston personally, as a member of her family or as a friend. Many, perhaps most of us here, will have met and known her in her own place, the Manor of Hemingford Grey. Those of us who weren't lucky enough to know her will wish to express our sympathy with the many people whose loss is immediate and personal. But there is another congregation, a much larger one in numbers, which would wish to share in this celebration of Lucy Boston's life. Most of them cannot be here in person, because they are scattered all over the world. They are her readers. As someone who to my own lasting regret never met Lucy Boston face-to-face, I should like to speak a brief word for that larger, affectionate but absent congregation who know the Manor of Hemingford Grey as the Yew Castle, and Yew Hall, and especially as Green Knowe, and who knew Lucy Boston as the grandmother, as Mrs Oldknow, and of course as the unique authorial voice.

I say 'knew', but the past tense here is happily inappropriate and unnecessary. Although the life is over, the work is still there. Although a memorial service is inevitably a kind of leave-taking, the task of someone speaking about the books is no such thing. Rather, it's a matter of speaking on behalf of the future, and on behalf of all the readers — especially the children — whose meetings with Lucy Boston have yet to happen, through the medium of Mrs Oldknow and her house.

In fact, the very nature of this occasion is itself a kind of comment on the themes and beliefs, and the great strengths, of Lucy Boston's books. We are all thinking this afternoon of a very long life. But Lucy Boston as a writer was always the sharpest corrector of any inclination on the part of her readers to measure time-scales by a single life's allotted span, however long. She would be indignant with us if she caught us treating a mere ninety-seven years as a long time. We should be on the receiving end of some astringent comments, I suspect. When we think of Hemingford Grey, of Green Knowe, we are thinking of nearly a thousand years, not a mere hundred, and thanks to her own efforts and those of her family Hemingford Grey is alive in stone for the future, and Green Knowe alive in language.

'O my house,' says Roger d'Aulneaux in *The Stones of Green Knowe*, 'live for ever'. Nothing lives quite for ever, as Lucy Boston very well knew and often reminded us. But when something is precious, you guard it as well as you can, for as long as you can. Her physical guardianship of the Manor is there for everyone to see. But guardianship is just as significant a theme in her books as it was in the practical activities of her life. The responsibility of the individual being is one of care, respect and intelligent transmission — from the past to the present, from the present to the future. That is one of several reasons why the house is so often and so beautifully called 'The Ark'. In a spendthrift and destructive age, it was Lucy Boston's triumphant achievement to make images of continuity so vivid as to win the imagination of children.

In *Yew Hall*, the narrator speaks of the time when the house was being restored, and of her thoughts — 'gliding tired but happy over the shape of the new life that I was to live, the shape, that is, of the house itself in its island setting ... for already I had realised and accepted my destiny, which was to be the temporary vessel of the consciousness of the long, unremembered life of the house.' That consciousness of inheritance, stewardship and transmission is the special property of Mrs Oldknow. If it were hers alone the books might seem didactic, which they do not. They may seem wedded to a conservationist morality, which in part they certainly are, and rightly so. But only in part, because the appeal of the books is more powerfully to imaginative vision than to moral insight. That sense of being a temporary vessel of the house's consciousness is conscious knowledge for Mrs Oldknow, but for the children, it is magical discovery. This is so for Tolly in the twentieth century, for Toby, Alexander and Linnet in the seventeenth, and above all perhaps for Roger d'Aulneaux, almost a full millennium ago. When the young Roger is moved through time with the help of magic stones to the twentieth century, he sees the grandmother in the garden of the house, and realises that he is seeing in her old age one of his own descendants. When as a child reader you understand that, and understand its delight and importance, you have begun to understand time. You can start to see why ninety-seven years is only a moment.

The poet Philip Larkin wrote:

> Truly, though our element is time,
> We are not suited to the long perspective
> Open at each instant of our lives.

But Lucy Boston is pre-eminently suited to the long perspectives, and her originality has much to do with that. She is completely identified with one house and one small place, but out of it she made a world. She wrote, 'I believe that one place closely explored will yield more than continents passed through. Now I have found the place I need, and this is where I stay, getting deeper in it every moment and always surprised'. But when she said of herself 'I am not a traveller', she was only right in the most literal sense. A great deal of travelling took place from the Manor at Hemingford Grey. There is travelling in time, back through the generations of the Oldknow family, and further still, to earlier houses on the site and then to the prehistoric fantasy of *The River at Green Knowe*. There is travelling in space, from the Music Room, or the Knight's Hall, to the garden which merges imperceptibly with the house, and to the wood where Hanno hides, and across the moat, and to the fens, the river and the waterways that take you to the Wash, and so to the sea where earlier Oldknow generations made their living. There is travelling across ethnic boundaries, to the West Indian boy Jacob in the eighteenth century and the Chinese boy Ping in the twentieth. Most radical of all there is travelling across the boundary of species. Lucy Boston declared her belief that 'man-centred conception of life was false and crippling', that the lives of other creatures create great riches of ours, and in *The Stones of Green Knowe* and *A Stranger at Green Knowe* she gave that belief expression, with unforgettable imaginative power. The story of Hanno and Ping in *A Stranger at Green Knowe* is probably the finest achievement in modern children's fiction, and the book's visionary intelligence grows more timely and urgent for us every day. But all Lucy Boston's work is of a piece, unified by its wide and liberating perspectives of time and space and life-forms. Perhaps we should adjust her modest vision of herself as the transient vessel of consciousness for the house, and say that the partnership was a more equal one. The Manor at Hemingford Grey provided her with a language, a wonderful expressive instrument for her own uncompromising insights. It enabled her to follow in her own life and work the precept she valued so much and used to such effect in *An Enemy at Green Knowe*: 'Be thou that which thou art, and that which thou willest to be.'

⌘

(First published in *Signal*, January 1991)

Ian Kellam

Wine from a Rose — a Memory of Lucy M. Boston

It was June, 1967. I had written an opera for the boys of St John's College School, Cambridge, where I was at that time teaching. My friend, Brian Jordan — who, with Anne his wife, was the mainstay of the instrumental accompaniment to that piece — asked another friend of his, Lucy Boston, along to one of the performances. I remember Brian telling me that I might find her an interesting woman to meet, but at the time it was 'in one ear, out the other', as the expression goes.

Certainly I had forgotten all about her by the end of the performance. There was always much to do — instruments to put away, music to collect up and put back into order, boys to shoo away or employ as chair-stackers, as well as tidying up in general. Little time for social niceties. I learned, later, that Lucy had waited to speak to me. No one told me at the time, and I remember feeling annoyed that an old lady had been left standing about for so long. But that soon passed; I had met many an old dear in my time, one less was little loss.

The following day Lucy wrote to me. An enchanting letter, warm, friendly, and so generous in compliment that I immediately felt quite wretchedly guilty, and straightaway telephoned her to say so. She invited me to a performance at the Arts Theatre the following Thursday, and suggested we should meet over a sherry for a chat, beforehand.

I clearly remember wondering at the wisdom of a *second* sherry. This pale and somewhat unsteady old lady, in her navy blue silk dress and coat, reminded me so much of Great Aunt Lily, who lived in perpetual Victorian dusk, and who provided rock-cakes and weak tea to while away the tormented hours of those obligatory childhood visits. The vision was further compounded when I shepherded her into her seat, and later into the stately, elderly car she used as a taxi. . .

. . . Except that this old lady had bright black eyes that seemed to be searching through to the back of my scalp. . . and she didn't smell at all like Great Aunt Lily.

Still, I walked back to my rooms wondering why I had accepted her invitation to sacrifice a perfectly good weekend in her company, and at her house.

Like Shakespeare's unwilling schoolboy, heavy-footed along the path by the river at Hemingford, peering furtively over the wall and turning often to gaze enviously at a couple sculling up the placid river, I eventually found myself looking over a large and lovely garden — roses everywhere, huge flower beds, dipping lawns, and a path lined with stately topiary rising gently towards what looked like an intriguing and interesting old house. Except for a gardener, there was no-one in sight. For a moment I wondered if this might possibly be it; she'd said there was a garden . . . But fortune was never so kind, never so generous. . .

No, my old lady would live, like Great Aunt Lily, in a tiny semi-detached Victorian villa further on, with rust velour curtains, open just wide enough to let a chink of north light in and onto a grey aspidistra in a great yellowy-green cabbage of a pot on an unlovely Edwardian plant stand, shielding from sun and fresh air the shiny walnut suite with its upholstery of scratchy black horse hair. Inside there would be an aroma of cold linoleum and well-boiled cauliflower.

But there was nothing further on.

As quietly as I could, I opened the gate. It sagged a little, squeaked, and the sneck made a sharp noise as I lifted the little gate back into position. Nobody appeared, and the gardener did not appear to have heard. I made my way across to the bronzed, denim figure kneeling in the iris bed, strong gardener's hands vigorously at work, separating the tubers. Even when she sensed my nearness and rose to greet me, brushing the soil from her hands, I still had no idea. My bewilderment must have been obvious for she laughed outright as she took my hand. Black eyes dancing, black eyebrows signalling impish delight, she chuckled quietly, musically.

'I'm only really myself *here*, you see.'

It was the first of many astonishments to come. The 'old lady' evaporated (but was to reappear on a few occasions when she later came to see me in London, or when we went to concerts together. Her anxiety to get home again was obvious, and she never would stay the night). Although more than forty years separated us, I was never again to think of any age-gap. Except for a natural dignity, she was lively teenager or mature young woman, as it suited her. It was as natural to see her clambering upstairs as it was for me to follow on behind, puffing a little.

And so began a long and lovely chapter of delights. Her enthusiasm for all things that mattered, all our mutual interests, and more, was infectious. I cannot be the only one to be awakened to something new and interesting, time and again, by Lucy. It became the norm to be telephoned regularly and be expected to know, note for note, a piece of music she might have first heard that morning, or to discuss a book published the week before, or to have visited a newly-opened exhibition of the work of someone I had barely heard of, much less knew. In a way, one was bludgeoned into widening and expanding one's experiences. But — and of course — such widening and expansion was never anything less than exhilarating.

She even managed to kindle in me an interest in gardens. Up to that time gardens were, for me, akin to zoos; places to visit, and enjoy to a certain extent, but the one did not contain the pimpernels, dog-violets, ox-eye daisies, heathers and etc., of the meadows, fields and moors I loved, while the other unfortunately did contain the otters I would rather see at play in a Scottish river. She made me aware of flowers and plants I never knew existed. Up to that time an iris was an iris, blue or white, or sooty purple if in the front patch of a terraced house in Sheffield. So what were these majestic creations in coffee and cream, lime shading to lemon, sky-blue deepening to indigo? And the roses! Such roses! Had she never heard of, or seen, the roses of London front gardens — those neatly ranked balls of orange and flame atop stilt-straight foster-parents? No perfume there to interfere with the fumed air.

So what were these joyous, rambling profusions, with scent enough to stun? Today, I cannot put my nose into the multi-layered crimson-purple robes of Cardinal Richelieu without seeing again her face looking up into mine, eager for reaction. It was the first rose she handed me. Another favourite is the white climbing rose in the kitchen garden. I do not know its name, but on summer evenings, late, when the moon is high and there are lights from the house, this rose can glisten into an explosion of Leonids.

She led me around her garden that first afternoon — through the roses, around the topiary sculptures, by the bamboos, under trees, into Watson's 'preserves', through and under the calming wilderness on the wild side of the moat, and so on, until it was time for tea. By then I was breathless. Of course, we had talked non-stop, and by then Lucy had not only put me completely at my ease, but had made me feel somehow part of the place — an old and valued friend. She never lost the quiet capacity for giving, and inspiring, a generous love.

Tea was in the bower by the dipping front lawn (where, she told me, she had once found a carp flapping about after a flood, and which she had carried back to the river). We drank Orange Pekoe, from eighteenth-century Worcester porcelain tea bowls — another mild astonishment; such were usually behind glass, untouchable.

Later, while she prepared supper she left me, with typical sensitivity, to wander about the upstairs of the house alone. She must have smiled and chuckled to herself as she imagined my widening eyes and mouth. Now, a quarter of a century later, that first impression is still as vivid and fresh as then. It is still the most exactly *right* house I know; it bewitches immediately, and with every successive visit the tighter are you bound up in its spell and atmosphere. Its story is told — eloquently, as only Lucy can, in her book *Memory in a House* — but what she doesn't tell, in so many words, is of the stamp and impact of her powerful personality and imagination.

It is as though the house responded to her touch, and began to breathe again. Lucy and the house were as one, welded, wedded. Certainly the house spoke through Lucy. Later, she told me she felt she knew the Manor from an earlier time. She was quite matter-of-fact about it, and spoke with such simple conviction and quietude that the finger down my spine told me it was a mysterious truth.

It was not until I was in my room, exhilarated, wonderfully replete and exhausted, that I remembered I had left my weekend bag exactly where I had first been greeted by Lucy. But it was in the porch, by the sink that is ever chock-a-block with flowers (which, as likely as not, will be in a battered, but early, Derby vase, or in a glass inside a Roman pottery one, jostling shoulder to shoulder with humbler containers). Watson had found it.

After that weekend, I left carrying three of her books, and Lucy was part of my life.

Visits to the Manor became frequent and regular. Occasionally, there were other friends at the house — Mary Potts, Elisabeth Vellacott, John Guest, who I already knew through Mary and Harold Wilson, Elizabeth Poston, my friend Philip Grout, Enid Bagnold, or Lucy's brother, and there were evening gatherings when another great friend of hers, Colin Tilney, would electrify us with performances of the harpsichord works of Bach, Frescobaldi, and other early composers. But as often as not, Lucy and I would be alone, and on the whole I think she preferred this one-to-one relationship with all her friends.

A particular pleasure was the winter evenings when, after supper, and with a glass or two of good wine still to be poured from the bottle, we would sit either side of the huge open fire, cosy and comfortable, and chat, or listen to records. Lucy would watch with interest as I made my after-dinner roll-up, and once asked me to make one for her. But it was soon handed back with a distasteful look, as she reached for one of her Sobranie Black Russian cigarettes instead. In the early days of our friendship Lucy smoked sparingly and later not at all, as far as I know. Usually, on those evenings, she would be at work on her patchwork, as there was nothing she could do in the garden. It also freed her mind to plan and ponder the next day's work on her current book. These were always written during the winter; the summer months were given over to the demands of the garden. I marvelled not only at her instinctive mastery of design and colour sense, but also at the number of tiny stitches she managed to sew along each side of the small hexagons.

Music was powerfully important to Lucy, and early music most important of all, but this did not exclude a lively interest in, and appreciation of, the music of today. On one visit I took along my friend from boyhood, Max Davies (Sir Peter Maxwell Davies). She was clearly fascinated by him, and it was a satisfying pleasure to see each respond so readily to the other. Thereafter, on each visit, I was asked for the latest news of Max, and I would sometimes take with me his latest recording. Lucy would listen, engrossed, and there would be a lively discussion afterwards. For the most part she would be intrigued and appreciative but she could be sharply critical if she disliked anything — of his, mine or anyone else's, and her most telling criticism was silence . . .

Some years after we first met I wrote a children's book of my own. I had kept its writing a secret from Lucy, partly as a surprise (her name is in the dedication), but also from slight apprehension; one could never be certain of Lucy's reactions. However, it had received good press reviews, so, with a degree of confidence, I sent a copy to her. (I must say I was inordinately proud of it at the time, and longing to hear her praise.) It had already been arranged that I should go up to the Manor for another visit some three or four days after that, so off I went, all expectation.

Eventually, after lunch, she said, 'It was a marvellous idea — that metamorphosis of the boat — I wish I'd thought of something like that . . . quite a literary *coup* . . .' Pleased as Punch, I waited. And I waited. Then, '. . . and what are you writing at the moment?' She meant music.

Many years later, I sent her the typescript of another book. It was at the time her sight was beginning to fail, and reading it had obviously taken time and effort, but she was wonderfully kind and thorough about it, and wanted her son, Peter, to illustrate it.

Meals with Lucy were always a delight. Everything

was always just right, from the refreshingly simple, to the simply incredible, and one lunch in particular I can only describe as downright wicked.

I had driven from London for a brief — two-hour — chat, about a project we were both involved in. After that, I needed to rush back for a rehearsal. Soup was handed through the hatch for me to put on the table. Lucy appeared with a bottle of dark sherry, and poured a good glass into my portion, rather less into her own. I frowned slightly, while she, eyes alight and dancing, explained, 'It's so much nicer on a cold day like this.' After that came roast wild boar — from Harrods, or Fortnum's, I forget which — with what must have been horribly expensive new potatoes, asparagus, and spicy red cabbage. All to be washed down with a quite magnificent, almost black, Corton.

Deep in discussion, I didn't notice for quite a while that my glass never seemed to get any emptier. But it *was* good. Perhaps two and a *half* hours, then — and a strong black coffee; I should still just manage it. Huge logs crackled and flared in the hearth. How warm and comfortable it was. Then jelly and cream appeared. I've never much cared for jelly; such unpleasant greens and unnatural reds. But this looked quite interesting; deeper than garnets, almost as dark as the Corton. Moreover, tongue and palate tingled. Jelly was never like this in Sheffield, even swimming in tinned and squashed mandarin oranges...

Eventually, 'Wossinit?... Ho... Howjamaikit?' I heard myself ask, carefully.

'It's so simple,' said Lucy, 'just jelly and a bottle of port — oh, and a little cinnamon.'

I stared at the gently oscillating glass bowl. The cranberry tinge to its clear glass sides did nothing to disguise its emptiness.

Later that night, after a light supper — just soup, but this time without sherry, and a selection of cheeses — Lucy and I again sat opposite one another by the fire. We were talking again. 'I *knew* it would take longer than two hours,' she said, in that droll and mildly admonishing way of hers. But I was still there — I have to own — as much through my own epicurean greed as through her impish machinations. She knew me well by that time.

On another summer's morning — more accurately, half-way through the night, at first crack of dawn — Lucy shook me awake and handed me my dressing-gown. I think she had decided that no composer worth his salt could hope to attain the ivory tower's heights without having first heard the Dawn Chorus. Still half wondering if the place was afire, I was too bleary-eyed to say that I'd heard one once before, and that it hadn't helped, and that on many a morning I slammed the pillow over my head in an attempt to get beck to sleep. So I rose and followed dutifully.

Already the garden was awash with the songs of whales — those curiously eerie, upsetting, wonderfully hair-raising sounds, arcing and swooping through the half-light, coming from the gramophone through the open French windows of the sitting room. 'It's to encourage them,' explained the inventive Lucy, as if the noisy little brutes needed any encouragement. I was led from bush to shrub, from tree to briar to thicket, and back again, the better to distinguish the various orchestral sections tuning up. One — it might have been the finches — or was it the robins? . . . I forget — I was already deafened and numbed — kept us waiting an inordinately long time. Dew on the grass, damp in my slippers, I nodded and smiled a pantomime of interest as she advised me what next to listen for. So confident was she into thrilling me into breathless awe at this miracle, I'm quite sure she never guessed that I could cheerfully have shot the lot, including the gramophone. *They* knew, the wretches. Getting back to sleep was impossible; they flocked and crowded outside my window, their playground, shrieking with bright-eyed glee.

There are many instances of Lucy's thoughtfulness and sensitivity. One small memory comes to mind.

I rarely left the Manor without an armful of flowers in spring or summer, always containing some she knew I particularly liked. One cold April day I was arrested at the front door by a carpet of fritillaries under the music room window. One of my most favourite of wild flowers, I never expected to see them here, and so at home. I was thrilled, and crouched down to lift and look into one of the pale green bonnets, with its speckling of rust. When I stood up, Lucy was at the door, smiling with pleasure. 'I potted some for you, earlier,' she said. And there they were, on the board by the sink.

I could not help but feel, sometimes, that her enthusiasms, her animation, and her interests in so much, and all so robustly expressed, often challengingly, were in some way a honing and polishing of me. Each of us chooses friends with great care, but Lucy seemed to select hers with the same deliberation she might give to deciding which word was exactly right for that particular slot in a phrase, or which rose right for that particular corner of the garden. Subsequently, there was the pruning, the cutting down, and tending, all to the same purpose.

When that planned brief visit turned into an overnight stay, we were working together on an opera, the libretto for which she was adapting from one of her finest achievements, *A Stranger at Green Knowe*. Before I read the book I had noticed a photograph of Guy, the London Zoo's magnificent gorilla, pinned over the hatch through to the kitchen, and discovered that we had a mutual admiration and sympathy for that sad creature.

When I was asked to write another children's opera, this time for another school, and was sounding out Lucy for ideas, she came up with the idea of adapting *A Stranger*. I pointed out that what was wanted was something that could involve *all* the children, but that was to be no problem; after the principle characters, the 'other' children were to be the chorus and would play trees, bamboos and so on. Lucy swept all else aside and launched into the project with her usual vigour and commitment. As it happened there *was* only one real part for a child, that of Ping; and most of the others, Hanno (silent of course), Mrs Oldknow, and so on, were to be played by members of the teaching staff. Length alone gave to the part of Ping a role that would tax many a professional, let alone a schoolboy. What had been wanted was a half- or three-quarter hour piece, but Lucy's libretto was for a three-act opera of goodly length. It was far too good to be chopped down (and Lucy was so enthusiastic, and so gripped by the project that I could not bring myself to suggest it) and bursting with imaginative detail. It would still make a good chamber opera. But not for schools.

So it was almost a relief to me when the commissioning school wrote to abandon the project, saying they could no longer afford the fee. Lucy, however, was greatly disappointed, and her disappointment lasted over many months. By the time it was abandoned I had set one scene — where Ping discovers Hanno in the thicket. Later, when the cellist, Boris Heller, was invited to give a recital at Kettles Yard, Cambridge, with myself as accompanist, I adapted and arranged that scene into a work for cello and piano, and called it *The Boston Suite*. Lucy enjoyed the whole recital, and was intrigued by the piece, but I was 'ticked off' about its title — it was to be called *The Green Knowe Suite*.

Lucy kept a constant supply of nuts and seed for the garden's wildlife, so to be entertained over lunch by squirrels and birds playing and feeding outside the glass doors was almost commonplace. Because of this, cats were not tolerated at the Manor whereas well-behaved dogs were welcomed. In 1983, when I thought he was ready, I took my young English bull-terrier, Worcester, with me. Lucy thoroughly approved of him; she enjoyed his muscular solidity, and his ready smile kept her in constant chuckles. Worcester, who approves of anything and anybody (and whose favourite occupation is in washing any resigned local cat) was happy to turn approval to devotion for this nice lady — and her interesting cheese board. Once that sat upon the table he was solicitous in his attentions. She could not move without him moving with her. He sat by her chair, stock still, unblinking, head up and pointing, his powerful fluence directed at the cheese.

It was a warm day in late spring. The doors into the garden were wide open. A couple of squirrels, bolder than most but prudent enough to stay above ground level, flattened themselves against the lower branches of the great yew tree which almost brushes the house, and glared in at the dog, chattering angrily. He totally ignored them. Then a single thrush dropped down and stood in the doorway. After a few moments it advanced into the room. Worcester turned his head to look at it. Breathless, we watched, expecting it to take flight, but apart from some feather-tightening it stood its ground. Worcester turned back to more pressing matters. The bird came on to within a few inches of the dog. It stayed many moments, looking up at the three of us in turn before turning and flying off. The dog kept his gaze steady, burning through table and board. Lucy rocked with delight, and, of course, Worcester sampled each cheese. He has a quirk of transferring whatever remains of interesting tastes on his tongue, to a left foreleg, which he then licks for minutes on end, eyes closed, until the last vestige of flavour has disappeared. He is rarely without one clean leg. This never failed to intrigue Lucy and it was more or less required that Worcester came with me on each subsequent visit.

Colin Tilney housed one of his fine harpsichords in the rarely used room at the front of the house, overlooking the lawn. Sometimes I would play it for Lucy, usually Bach or Handel suites (though without Colin's skill and dexterity). Lucy would stand looking down at me, her hands resting lightly on the instrument's case. It was difficult to concentrate on the music without being distracted by those magnificent eyebrows semaphoring wildly over delighted eyes. Many a time have I broken down with mirth (well, it's as good an excuse as any) and asked her to sit by my side instead and turn the music.

There was so much joy in being with Lucy; there are so many crammed pleasures to recall — enough, almost, to aching point — that it seems odd to me that one particular, and very different, ache should linger so intrusively amongst the overall happy haze of memory. I don't remember the time of year, or the year itself, except that it must have been some time in the mid '70s. I had tried to telephone, but without success. There was nothing particularly unusual in that; she was more often than not in the garden on fine days, often until late into the evening. But telephoning regularly over several days, without answer, was odd, remembering how much she was loath to be away from home for more than a few hours. I was on the point of getting into the car when she answered.

She told me, very quietly, that she had been to France. For some reason, I felt disturbed. Trying to put my finger on it, I sank brightly into the usual daft platitudes — 'Did you have a nice time?!' and so on. Her answers were courteous, brief, and non-committal. Now I was really troubled, and selfishly wondered if I had unwittingly offended her, and how could I repair the damage. It didn't occur to me that someone else might be at the root of it. Then, after long moments of silence, she said, still quietly, 'When are you coming over?' 'Whenever you like...' There was more silence. '... Now?', I eventually suggested.

It was late afternoon when I set off and settling into dark by the time I arrived. She gave me her usual warm and smiling welcome but there was an unfamiliar heaviness about her. Much of the anticipatory pleasure of going to the Manor was her radiance, but even that seemed dimmed. I had taken some fruit — plums and nectarines, I think — which she simply left in the carrier, in the kitchen. That, too, was oddly unlike her. I remember little more until later on in the evening when we were sitting opposite one another again, she in her usual chair to the right of the wide ingle with its funnelling chimney open to the sky. On sunny days you can watch the silhouettes of planes passing over yesterday's ashes. She had said very little during the evening: it was not that she was uncommunicative; she just said very little, and even more quietly than usual. The journey had tired her, naturally, but there was clearly more to it than that. Her mind was elsewhere.

At last, I asked her to tell me about her trip. She said she had been to see a friend, someone in a monastic order. Her visits to the monastery had been limited, there was little to do or see in the local town, her hotel bed had been uncomfortable. She stared sadly into the fireplace, obviously still in France, then rose and went to the cupboard behind me, and handed me, without comment, a drawing.

It was of the fine and sensitive face of a young man, with a Renaissance beauty about him. I had already sensed that I was beginning to understand. This confirmed it. I knew the drawing was by Lucy (and I was — as usual — astonished by the sureness and sensitivity of her line, another branch of her talents. Painting is one thing, drawing another). I restricted myself to commenting only on this drawing, leaving her to tell me about its subject as and when she felt. For a long time she was silent, then gave me a long, sad, half-smile, saying, 'He's in his thirties . . .' Another pause, '. . . I'm in my eighties."

There was nothing for me to say, and, I think, nothing wanted. For the moment, the only understanding and sympathy I could offer — and that in waves — was silence. I had never seen, or felt, such pain and sadness in another, and I shall be happy never to see or feel it again. I left her alone while I washed up the two plates and glasses, found the fruit and put it into its bowl, and made coffee. Later, she unburdened herself, with her usual quiet dignity, and, I hope, felt a little eased for doing so.

Although I was deeply touched — and more moved than I can convey — that she should share such a confidence with me, I don't think it was especially me she wanted to tell; I just happened to telephone at that time. I believe that she really wanted to be alone, but that, perhaps, it was a little easier for her to feel more safely alone when another sat in the other chair. I think Lucy loved as passionately as she lived — more committed, more completely than most. Being who and what she was, and with the advantage of the gifts of both articulate expression and wisdom, she could to a certain extent tell her thoughts in prose and poetry — '... the bomb of love . . . exposing age's climb to loneliness', 'Whom time will not reprieve', etc. — and in the garden, too, there was solace.

But ultimately, I believe her greatest comfort lay in the strongest and most understanding of arms — those the house held out.

There is a time in the early dusk of a summer's evening when all the perfumes of the garden seem to be at their headiest, when wildlife and house prepare for the night, and, apart from a snatch of evensong from a solitary blackbird, night sounds come mostly from far away across the river. Then, there is nothing more pleasant than simply to chat idly, and to think. Many a time have Lucy and I sat in the garden, relaxing over a bottle of hock, but drinking it from a white rose, however close-petalled — her delightful whim at that time — can be a touch messy; it does tend to run down fingers, shirt and trousers. Nevertheless, the memories of those evenings spring readily to mind and I often find myself smiling, looking at nothing, except perhaps a mental picture of that animated face, those large black eyes under ever alert eyebrows.

A cynical, but otherwise intelligent young friend (I never learned if his ambition for political life was ever fulfilled, but I expect it probably was) once remarked that Lucy had 'lost touch with the real world', and that her books and her house were 'escapist'. So they are, but he was too old in one sense and too inexperienced in another, to understand how or why.

As for losing touch, Lucy was more acutely in touch with reality than most; her sensitivity made her all the more 'aware' of the real world. I think it is why, all those years before, recognising the permanence, and impervious serenity of the house, she made of it a place where the old-fashioned truths of gentleness, beauty and understanding were not so much against that 'real' world as an island within it, there for anyone to visit and to be refreshed from the shoddy, the unlovely, the mass-produced.

Long before Conservation became the issue it is today she spoke to me with her usual quiet passion of her fears for the destruction of forests and wildlife, of Man's uncomprehending madness. Like many of us, fearful of the consequences of rain-forest decimation and worse, acid rain, and so on, she felt for the most part impotent as to what she could personally contribute to the broad canvas of protest, so was all the more determined to preserve what she had created and tended, as her statement, her example.

And over the astonishingly productive last three and a half decades of her life she was to magic the house and garden into the sanctuary we know, still the still Guardian of those original ideals, and now Keeper of the atmospheric mysteries of other aurelian truths: fiction is fact, and past present. There is the 'real' and the Real.

On the wall facing me as I sit at my desk, is a felt-covered board. Pinned over the greater part of it are papers mostly relating to work, and, down one side, photographs. I have been so fortunate throughout my life in meeting and coming to know, through work or accident, many outstanding originals. Amongst them there is Stanley Spencer, scowling pugnaciously from under his old black umbrella, and Noel Coward, gazing admiringly at a bronze bust of himself. Both are posed, each is characteristic of the man.

And there is a photograph of an empty room. Sunlight floods through Norman arched windows and door, throwing into silhouette ancient oak beams and buttresses. Candles and candlesticks abound, notably two of curved and polished wood which at first glance could be likened to climbing, fighting salmon. Although I cannot see it, there is a Norman fireplace to my left. Above it sit other candlesticks, of brass, which are never left to tarnish and to which centuries of polishing have given that unmistakable patina.

All suggest evenings when the room takes on another character, another warmth, when rugs and sofas are covered with people, sitting, half lying, propped up on elbows, curled in corners, all listening, while the glow from the many candles and the big Chinese lantern melds faces and stone into one, and times past and present are indistinguishable one from the other. But at the moment, and forever, the room is as empty as its history will allow, crammed only with summer, so that I can walk in and cross over to the sofa by the far wall and sit, carefully, so as not to disarrange too much its loose patchwork covering, and where I can be alone and at the same time number amongst the thousands.

For these moments it is *my* room. But I shall quite understand if you who know it, know it as *your* room. Indeed, I should expect it; it is that sort of room. Lucy was that sort of person.

Again, it is a photograph which could be said to have been posed, in that furniture and objects have been positioned by she who restored dignity and life to it. It is as characteristic of her as the pose of any of the other faces around it. Pasted to a card which is now brown and flaking, scorched with age, the picture is as clear as the memories it evokes, and as evocative as Lucy's hand, where, on the back, she has written, *Semper stat ibidem.*

I do not need a photograph of Lucy herself. While the face of Great Aunt Lily is as a wraith in the mist, Lucy's springs readily to mind, clear as through Cornish air, glowing as richly as her paintings, her patchworks, and her beloved roses, and as near in memory as her books are close to hand. Memories jostle and crowd, as alive and joyous as an abundance of bees in summer. She was not only the most remarkable woman I ever knew, but one of Life's rarities — a complete person.

As I said at the beginning, Lucy gave and inspired a generous love, and had that extraordinary and rare capacity for making you feel that only you mattered, that only you cared, appreciated and understood. I, like every one of her friends, loved her very much.

Below that last photograph is a quotation from Zoltan Kodaly, which has been by my desk since I was a student. It reads, 'No one is too great to write for children; in fact, he should try to become great enough to do so.'

Lucy Boston did just that, and she became great.

⌘

Frances Linehan

(aged 12 when she wrote this)

I first met Lucy Boston when I was six, through her books, and for that year of my life that is how I knew her — as Mrs Oldknow. Even when I actually met her the resemblance between Lucy and Mrs Oldknow and her house and garden was so strong that it was impossible to know where one ended and the other began. In fact they were the same person. When I saw her I had the very same impression that seven-year-old Tolly received of his great-grandmother: 'short silver curls' and both their faces 'had so many wrinkles it looked as if someone had been trying to draw them for a very long time and every line put in had made the face more like her'. This was a perfect description of Lucy. But Tolly did not describe her eyes. On my first visit she told me to close my eyes then she put something into my hands. It was cold. I looked and it was Toby's mouse. As I looked from its life-sized ebony-black eyes to Lucy, I could see the connection. Both were so brilliant and alive; so very, very black, filled with mystery and secrets.

Lucy painted books and wove magic around herself, her house and her garden, and sewed it into her quilts. That caused you, on entering the garden, to enter a hemisphere of magic, tranquility and expectancy. Somehow everything was more real, and everyone was waiting, was tense, but in a good, important way. Many things from the books were on the walls and tables, so you were walking into a living story. While wandering around you would constantly be thinking how many others had worked, sat and laughed before, and how many still did. It was a wonderful feeling.

But my main memories of Lucy are centred around squirrels (they were black ones, Lucy could not have ordinary squirrels!) We spent a very happy time feeding them with nut chocolate and shouted with delight when they pressed their faces against the glass of the French windows to beg, then ran away to watch from a hiding place while we put out another square. No sooner was the window closed than the sqirrel was back again, delicately picking up the chocolate in its paws and running away to eat it in peace. It is my most alive and fresh memory of Lucy: her bright black eyes watching the squirrel as it stalked the chocolate. I felt like Tolly when he had his hands buttered to feed the birds.

I want to say that it was a long time ago that I became entangled in Green Knowe — in fact it was half my life ago. I was six and Lucy was ninety so I had missed most of her life, although I had heard the stories. I did not know her well. I met her a very few times and sent her postcards and sometimes a story and a picture, but I suppose lots of children who read her books did that. Now I only have to go back to the books and she is there again. She is Mrs Oldknow, Tolly's great-grandmother, or Linnet's, or Roger's —

the old lady in every story who knows so much and is not necessarily telling it all. I do not especially mean wise, just because she is very old, after all Lucy wrote *Perverse and Foolish*; I mean that she and they knew lots of things that everyone else never knew or has forgotten, about the really old ways before and outside history, the real magic that time did not matter, and she gives us a glimpse of them in the books. She was very lucky because she had a wonderful house and could get to know everyone in it. She made me know that time was not straightforward. Just as Tolly could hear a baby crying centuries before and was teased by Linnet, Toby and Alexander, just out of sight, I know that Lucy is still at Green Knowe. Although she has left this earth she is just round the corner, probably standing next to the yew deer in the dark cool under the trees — if I can be quick enough.

⌘

Richard Luckett

Memory, as Lucy wrote, is a known cheat. Forgetfulness is something worse, and it comes as a shock to discover that I do not remember when I first met Lucy. Yet in a way that is appropriate, since it was an essential feature of Lucy that she was always there, and always had been; at her funeral people could be heard saying, slightly bemusedly, that it was not an event they had ever foreseen themselves attending. But I do know that I was friendly with her before the 17th December, 1971, because on that day Michael Ramsey, the Archbishop of Canterbury, came to induct my father into the living of Cranbrook. During supper, in one of those shifts from apparent abstraction to detailed enquiry that were at first disconcerting, he asked me what I did. I replied that I taught at Cambridge, and when he went on to ask what I was interested in, said 'poetry and music'. This was followed by a prolonged silence, and, no doubt, other people's conversation. Then the Archbishop swung round to me once more, and said: 'You must know Lucy Boston.' I did. 'Ah,' said the Archbishop, as though this settled something. 'Good.'

It took twenty years for the full oddity of this conversation to dawn on me. It is vouched for by my mother, who had heard the talk of Lucy, and was greatly impressed by the Archbishop's immediate bulls-eye. So was I; it had not before occurred to me that Anglican Primates were versed in Zen Archery. What made it remarkable at the time was that one of the reasons I had immediately come to like and admire Lucy was that no one could have been less 'Cambridge'. I had been introduced to her by Mary Potts, who had not only firmly distanced herself from academic life but maintained an amused scepticism about it that was decidedly bracing. Lucy seemed to me to take the process a stage further, though I do not think that I could have rationalized it at the time. But I was certainly beginning to suspect that a characteristic assumption of the second half of the twentieth century, that universities represented the apogee of civilization and that they were in some way ultimate embodiments of cultural, intellectual and ethical values (if these things can really be separated), was not to be taken for granted and was perhaps even dangerous. When I first met Lucy only a couple of people whom I knew in Cambridge also knew her (in due course she was to be the occasion of making many new friends). Moreover the immediate aspect of her to strike me, and it was something that renewed itself at every subsequent encounter, was her passionate interest in things and people for their own sake, an interest that was at once intensely discriminating and at the same time by-passed or made irrelevant whole areas of futile preoccupation. After five minutes with Lucy one was no longer vexed with Dr Leavis (with whom I had recently tangled in print) or perplexed by Roland Barthes (only a cloud the size of a man's hand then, but one sensed the storm to come). Not that Lucy was oblivious to Cambridge Philistinism; perhaps only Mary's remarks on the vandalisation of King's Chapel were sharper than hers, and no one could have laughed more at a passage from a letter from the glass painter Henry Gyles of York, who made the royal arms in Trinity library and subsequently wrote, of the Fellows, 'Masters of Art? No greater enemies to Art!'

That Michael Ramsey should have divined anything of this would have been extraordinary. The real imponderable only emerged shortly before Lucy died, when I happened to say something based on the assumption that she had known him. She had never (and her memory was still crystalline) met him in her life. No plausible solution to this mystery has ever presented itself; *Memory in a House* had not yet been published and, for various reasons, the Archbishop's sister-in-law, Lettice, is unlikely to have been the point of contact. In later years, having shifted allegiances and become a Fellow of Ramsey's old college, I saw him often, but it never occurred to me to mention Lucy. With another Senior Fellow of Magdalene it was a different matter.

I met I.A. Richards in 1975. Lucy had first met him sixty years before. *The Winter's Tale* always seemed to me Lucy's play, not just for Perdita/Persephone, but because it was manifestly in her power to

'turne my glasse, and give my Scene such growing
As you had slept betweene . . .'

For the next eleven years, until Dorothea's death in 1986, my life was, for better or worse, bound up with the Richards' household. Had Lucy not met Ivor at Llyn

Ogwen I doubt that this would have happened. The account of that meeting in *Perverse and Foolish* is comical enough, but as Lucy told it, it was even funnier. When the Richards returned from the States to live permanently in Cambridge the fact that I knew Lucy was an instant passport to friendship. For some years one of the high points of each summer had been the day when they would go over to Hemingford on the bus, and Ivor and Lucy would read their poems 'under the tree'; reports of these occasions were the first clue I had that Lucy was a poet. After Ivor's death my relations with Dorothea took an unexpected direction best summed up by the modification she would make to medical forms, crossing out next-of-kin and substituting 'Guardian on behalf of the College'. This unilateral appointment was not without its *sturm und drang* (liberally laced with farce) and would not have been sustainable without Lucy's unwavering support... It was not that we spent time discussing Dorothea's foibles, though I expect I reported a few of the more remarkable, but that Lucy put the whole thing into perspective. Dorothea, she told me, had not changed in fifty years, and Ivor had been a saint. This was something of which I needed to be reminded. Of equal importance was Lucy's living proof that old age need not bring with it any diminution of clarity and wit, and that its infirmities can be borne with patience and without complaint. All of these things were, of course, embodied in the Manor itself, which came increasingly to be a place of refuge.

I had known Lucy for some time before I was invited to the Manor, but after my initial visit, invitations flowed, to musical evenings (and afternoons, sometimes), to parties, to lunch or dinner when Lucy was by herself. Every occasion was eagerly anticipated and never disappointed, and the same was also true (at least so far as I was concerned) of the times, which regrettably became increasingly infrequent, when I was able to persuade Lucy to come, usually for concerts, to Cambridge. There was no one with whom it was better to listen to music, not because of what she might say about it (very little) but because of the intensity of her enjoyment. I am not certain, however, that my impressions of the Manor as a building quite match other people's, a consequence once again of that slight but distinct modification of the ordinary laws of time and space that one began to take for granted in anything that involved Lucy. I knew a house in Gloucestershire at least as old as the Manor and to which much the same things had happened: around a high and deep walled Norman hall a seventeenth century farmhouse with a central arrangement of chimneys had been built, leaving round headed internal lights. Bury Court cannot, from its situation, have a moat, though it does have a vaulted undercroft, and though its gardens cannot compare with the Manor's they have been given care, and a wine-producing vine from stock grown by my father grows over one wall. I never told Lucy about it. But I could not refrain from exclaiming at the engraved pane by David Peace in the sash-window of the music room, since David had also engraved a similar pane for my Godfather's dining room in Nottinghamshire. And Colin Tilney's Woffington harpsichord, which had come to rest in the work-room, I had last seen in Kent when he was living in the sole remaining fragment of Surrenden Dering, a Jacobean mansion which had housed my prep-school, and the destruction of which by fire I had watched as a seven-year-old in the early hours of an October morning in 1952. In consequence, the Manor was instantly familiar — though not any more so than it would have been to someone (of a younger generation than mine) who had grown up on *Green Knowe*.

As a defence against cheating memory I made notes of some of my visits to the Manor, but though I am confident of their accuracy these now seem totally misleading. The record of what was eaten and drunk ('Champagne, artichoke soup, casseroled pork, Côtes du Rousillon, lemon soufflé, Lucy forgot she had made a salad, but we ate it with the cheese') and music played ('Froberger, all the metrically bizarre gigues quite perfect and an intrinsic part of an utterance, a wholly theatrical suite by Georg Bohm, four of the three-part inventions, the *Capriccio on the Departure of a Beloved Brother*, an absurd fantasia by C.P.E. Bach, and then C.P.E.'s rondo on parting with his Silberman clavichord', that, of course, was Derek Adlam, and I added that I 'had waited twenty years to hear the clavichord played like that, and that only the unique circumstances at Hemingford had made it possible'), and people present (Elisabeth, Mary, Howard Ferguson, Ron Lewcock, Trevor Beckerleg, grandchildren) sounds all too much like what exactly it was not: a meeting of the Wine and Food Society in the days of A.J.A. Symons and André Simon. Nothing could have been further removed. What held it and us together was love for Lucy, whom we all approached by our separate paths, diverse and distinct, rather as you might come to the Manor by the drive or from the river or through the orchard. Infinite trouble had been taken: 'I owe Derek a suitable audience' Lucy once wrote to me. Only now do I wake up to how complicated the business of orchestrating lifts must have been — Lucy specialized in car-less friends, of whom I was one. Here was a separate world, at every season of the year. I remember it on a Sunday evening in February of 1980. Mary Potts, Trevor Beckerleg and I went over because Colin was staying. The garden was partly flooded, the dark water so still that it reflected the stars, and the angular stance of the Manor as approached through the topiary chessmen particularly evident. So, too, was the sense of an enclave, its solitude gathered and defensive, the Huntingdon Road a ribbon of movement to the north-west and only one quarter of the horizon untainted by the reflected glow of neon lights.

Equally vivid is an evening in 1984 when the music room was so golden in the setting sun that Lucy did not light the candles. Afterwards Lucy refused to be helped with the serving, and, hands shaking a little, insisted on taking down a stack of six heavy earthenware dinner plates from a head-high cupboard and taking them into the dining room. The copper beech faded into the evening. We carried out the clavichord ('just like the undertaker's men on the stairs' said Lucy) into the last gleamings of twilight, the leaves and ivy and rose-bushes etched out against the sky. It had been such a cold May that until then I had not noticed how much the year had advanced.

Then something over a year later, at the end of June, going over by myself to find Lucy alone in the garden, where she had been all day with a photographer, we did what I have never done before, looked at all the roses carefully, and as we went Lucy picked the ones she liked best for me, until I had a great gathering of blooms: Damasks, Venus, Portland, Duchess of Montebello, Nonnerie with its pungent *anis* smell, Picardie, tea rose like the dregs in a cup, cabbage roses of architectural perfection. She had cooked moussaka and vegetables for supper. She quizzed me about Christianity and said 'if it works for you that's the only thing that matters', an option I thought I should have resisted had anyone else said it. We agreed about the faults in construction and *longeurs* of *Middlemarch*, Lucy being surprised when I said that I would not have been prepared to admit that as an undergraduate; she would have expected it to be the other way round (this in turn surprised me). We talked about mutual friends, one changed by a bereavement, one wholly unchanged. The latter had recently successfully undergone a cataract operation, a problem which concerned Lucy, who needed one but the specialist had refused to do it under just a local anaesthetic: 'so that's that'. She would not have a general anaesthetic; the only thing she feared now was becoming senile. As to things in general: they had got worse in her life-time.

In retrospect that remark seems out of character. No one could have sided more consistently with the young. No one, by their very existence, could have seemed more to contradict its presumptions. But I do not put it down to the dark quandary which Lucy had to face. She did believe that in matters of keeping faith, in apprehension of beauty, in courtesy, there had been a diminishment. About this she did not feel the least vindictive, and against it she entrenched herself with friends. When Mary Potts was dying of cancer in

Arthur Rank House I found the total lack of sentiment in Lucy's attitude disconcerting; it was, as I thought at the time, 'as though she had written Mary off. But what else is she to do?' The answer came a few months after Mary had died and Lucy was looking back on a bad year. 'Now Mary has gone I must make new friends.' This might imply that Lucy had a manipulative attitude to friendship. She did not. There were, I know, names that ceased to be mentioned, invitations that were not repeated, but that was that. And if Lucy bastioned herself with friends it was not something that we ever knew, even when she told us so.

There seemed to be so little one could do in return. About the only thing I did was occasionally go over and tune the Woffington. Tuning a harpsichord for one's own purposes is one thing; tuning for a professional and an audience is another, especially if one is of a nervous disposition. It was after I had tuned for Colin at the Fitzwilliam and he had said to me, with great kindness, 'interesting temperament you've put on this. What is it?' that I resolved not to do so again. But I must have made a mental reservation in favour of Lucy, and at the Manor it never went wrong, a phenomenon that can only be put down to the secret harmonies of the *genius loci*. It also afforded me my most striking memory of Lucy. I had gone into the house, as usual, and called out, but got no answer. The weather was too dreary for her to be in the garden. Eventually I found her in her bedroom, poring over Benedict Nicolson's monograph on Georges de la Tour. Which plate was it? The Dream of St Joseph? Job mocked by his wife? She was entranced. I could have burst a paper bag but to no avail. What I seemed to be looking at, as she sat there in the fading light, even her breathing invisible, was the latest and last de la Tour.

It was a duty, not a kindness, to introduce Lucy to Margaret Faultless, and it would be merely foolish to attempt to evoke Elisabeth's extraordinary painting of the afternoon when Maggie played to the apparently unconscious Lucy who, as Diana later told us, had taken everything in. All I can say is that when other people have described what they have felt when looking at the painting, they have described, quite precisely, the experience of having been there. But we knew that she had heard it all. Even when, after the stroke, Lucy was unable to speak if there was more than one person in the room, she would still begin to laugh before you had completed your sentence.

⌘

Margaret McElderry

The Children of Green Knowe was my introduction to Lucy Boston. And what an introduction the book was! Submitted to me by its originating British publisher as a possible venture for my list in the US, it brought me such a sense of excitement at the quality of the writing, the extraordinary freshness of the story's telling, the originality of the way in which the distant past and the present were blended in an ancient English manor-house setting, the seemingly effortless evocation of unforgettable characters that I had that rare and wonderful sense of holding a treasure in my hands that must, without a doubt, be shared with young American readers.

Not until some time later did I have an opportunity to meet Lucy Boston in person, during a business trip to England. The appointed day came. I was to go by train to Huntingdon and taxi to Hemingford Grey and the Manor (that one can only think of as Green Knowe) where Lucy lived. I approached the meeting nearly overwhelmed by awe. How could I, a relatively new children's book editor, possibly converse with someone whose gift of language and whose astute observations of humanity were so extraordinary? Furthermore, because of odd train schedules, I was to spend the night at the Manor, which extended the challenge over a considerable period of time.

Lucy and I sat, each in one of the big, comfortable chairs at either side of the huge Elizabethan fireplace in her dining room, having tea. The fire — coal and wood burning — blazed brightly. Tea was served in very old, very beautiful and fragile lustreware cups, and we talked. Or, as much as possible, I listened. Lucy told me some of the history of the Manor, how she had found it and, with the help of her architect and her son, Peter, restored it as far as possible to its original condition. And she told me of the ghosts and spirits of the house — some benign, some not. Her large, dark eyes gleamed in the firelight as dusk drew in. I found myself wondering uneasily if I could sleep a wink that night, such was the spell being woven. At last I mentally shook myself, saying, 'This is all very well, but you're an American and these ancient beings cannot hurt you.' Specious reasoning, if there ever was!

Night came, after a lovely dinner and evening, full of laughter and conversation — conversation, like all good ones, that wandered over all sorts of topics and ideas: books, people, personal experience. To bed we went, each armed with a hot water bottle, essential in this ancient place, with its thick stone walls. In a soft, welcoming bed, with beautiful, heavy linen sheets, I slept one of the best sleeps I've ever known — and over many subsequent years, that bed has always been a blessed one for me. Occasionally, I would sleep so long that Lucy would come in and sit on my feet to waken me in the morning.

Rich, treasured memories flood my mind as I think

back over the many years during which I was privileged to have Lucy as a friend. One of the high-lights of those years was my wedding which took place at St Margaret's church in the nearby village of Hemingford Abbots. Like my long friendship with Lucy, the wedding weekend — and everything to do with it — was punctuated with laughter at the many funny and unexpected things that happened. Lucy herself gave me away. A lovely champagne luncheon at the Manor followed the wedding ceremony and even though part of the kitchen ceiling had fallen the night before, just missing all the glassware laid out for the next day, and the old retired butler (from one of the Cambridge University colleges), who was brought in to help, arrived wearing a tail coat green with age and old spots from other festive occasions, the luncheon was a great success, thoroughly enjoyed by all. In Lucy's book, *Memory in a House*, there is a chapter describing some aspects of the wedding.

One other memory — a memory of the ridiculous — comes from Lucy's and my later years. It, too, celebrates the sense of humour that we so strongly shared. Lucy, by this time, used a walking stick when she was outside in her garden. I used one, too, because of my arthritic knees. On a bright day, we were in the garden, near the path along the River Ouse, separated from the garden by high hedges. Lucy turned too quickly to point something out, lost her balance and fell on her back before I could reach her. It was frightening, but she said at once that she was all right. Then ensued a struggle to get Lucy on her feet again. I pulled and she tried without any success. I suggested she turn over onto her hands and knees, if she could, and we would try again. 'I haven't been on my hands and knees since I was a baby,' she said forcefully, 'and I'm not going to try now!' We laughed helplessly — until help came in the form of a young US airforce officer who, walking along the river path, heard our laughing struggles and, at our invitation, came into the garden to help. He was not there by accident, it turned out. His wife was an ardent fan of Lucy's books and they had come to look at her house from the river path. Instead they had found Lucy herself and were given a tour of the house.

Lucy is so much alive in her remarkable books, in the minds of all children and adults in many parts of the world who have read them in English and in translations, in the hearts and memories of all who were lucky enough to know her, and in the Manor itself to this day, that one does not so much salute her memory but instead her indomitable spirit, seeking out new experiences, wherever they may be.

⌘

Gillian Newbery

Lucy's Patchwork

Lucy made at least nineteen patchwork bedcovers during her life-time. A couple of these made during the war contain pieces of furnishing fabric mixed with dusters, drying cloths and huckabuck face-cloths. Even with these utilitarian materials the finished covers are things of beauty.

She became very ambitious with her patchworks. The most astonishing thing about the mechanics of her quilts is not only the choice of really quite extraordinary and often what most people might regard as apparently unsuitable material but also the way she cut the template shape out of the fabric. With meticulous care each piece was carefully judged and planned so that the patterns in the fabrics were used to create new patterns in the patchworks. Her first masterpiece, the patchwork of the crosses, demonstrates this to perfection.

The patchwork of the heavens is worked out with mathematical precision, and where exactly the effect she wanted could not be achieved with the fabric, she embroidered stars. No time was spared to make it just right. She was a perfectionist.

Her kaleidoscope quilt demonstrates her artist's eye in the choice of each piece of fabric so that all the shapes flow into each other, creating a masterpiece of the art of patchwork. Every block of the black and white quilt is a work of art.

Her later quilts are so daring and different it is difficult to believe that they were done by the same person. The sunburst one with its hot, vivid madras checks and batiks is a patchwork of strong and vibrant colours. The quilt with the appliquéd birds and squirrels once again shows a courageous use of seemingly unsuitable but totally successful mix of materials. Each fabric is so carefully chosen that it achieves the exact texture of the creature for which it is used. The mattress ticking edge is inspired.

The mariner's compass quilt with each centre so carefully chosen and every point perfect is a triumph, particularly as by this time she was sewing in white thread in order to be able to see her stitches. In her final patchwork she used a mixture of needlecord and cotton giving a glow that almost has the look of a stained-glass window.

What a collection! Let it be an inspiration to all patchwork enthusiasts. It is astonishing that this was only a small part of Lucy's life, a life which had so many facets: her house, her books, her garden, her kindness to anyone who passed by and showed interest. Remarkable!

⌘

Philippa Pearce

I usually think of Lucy Boston in her garden and in her garden in her books. Once, strolling through Hemingford Grey with a friend, we reached Lucy's garden gate and — of course — looked over it. (This was some time after I had been properly introduced to her and been entertained by her.) I thought I would test the legend. There she was, in the middle distance, gardening, but — no doubt — with a sideways glance to spare, like a bird. I gazed that fraction of time longer than ordinary casual interest should allow and — sure enough — she stopped her gardening and flew up to us to ask if we would perhaps like — and then recognized me and haled us into the garden, anyway.

Inside the garden there were always special Bostonian things to see. Lucy showed my daughter (then a child) an old shed in which (she said) a ghost had got shut up. It wasn't there any more because she had heard it rapping at the window and had let it out. We peered, still rather fearfully, through cobweb-blinded windows. Then there was the little deer in the shrubbery, growing year by year under Lucy's hands, until one day it would be a full-grown piece of topiary work.

I remember particularly the hottest of summer afternoons, sitting in the garden with my husband, while Lucy was indoors preparing tea. We were facing the coronation topiary. The sun shone full on the yew and a blackbird lay on the slope of it with wings outstretched on either side, basking, ecstatic. I happened never to have seen such a sight before. When Lucy came from the house, I pointed out the blackbird to her. 'Oh, yes,' she said comfortably, unsurprised at whatever natural, supernatural or fictional might happen in her garden.

⌘

Olivia Rowe

(aged 11 when she wrote this)

All L.M. Boston's books about Green Knowe make you feel that you are travelling through time.

In *An Enemy at Green Knowe* there are lots of passages which could have been made very frightening, however, Lucy Boston makes them funny at the same time as making them creepy. It is this ability to see two very different sides of the same story which attracts me. I had read all the stories about Green Knowe before I was ten years old.

When Tolly comes to Green Knowe for the first time, the eyes of the people in the painting follow him as he crosses the room. When you think about it in scientific terms it is impossible, yet when reading the book it seems as natural as breathing. You get the feeling that if you looked over the top of the book the characters would be in the room with you.

As you are reading the book you try to imagine what is going to happen next. Nearly always you are wrong, but what happens is always more exciting.

When you finish reading any of L.M. Boston's books you have the enormous satisfaction at everything turning out all right at the end.

⌘

Judy Taylor

More than twenty years have passed since Lucy Boston dedicated *Nothing Said* to me but I remember clearly how it came about. I had been in hospital and Lucy wrote me a letter to cheer me up. I came across it just the other day, dated July 1968, and what a typical letter it is. 'We have had, following the gale which brought down several trees, the worst floods since 1947, and in mid-summer. I spent much time in gum boots taking photos of my new water garden. It was a foot deep and looked intentional and really very handsome! I fear the irises will all be rotten. There's not a flower left anywhere, but a visiting child was able to pick a saucer full of wild strawberries that were under glass-clear water 'real Green Knowe stuff!'

I was so enchanted with the picture this conjured up that I suggested to Lucy she might put it into her next book. Reluctant to write another Green Knowe story, perhaps feeling that the saga was then complete (it was not for another eight years that she was to write *The Stones of Green Knowe*), she wrote instead a slip of a book which had only 58 pages and cost £1 — and was dedicated to me.

Nothing Said (Faber 1971) is about an only child, Libby, who goes to stay with a young friend of her parents' while they are at a conference. The house is not, unexpectedly, very unlike Green Knowe, with its garden bordered by a river, and when the floods come the garden is submerged beneath the water. 'As Libby sat on her stone ledge and looked at herself in the water ... she suddenly noticed below down by her feet, some dark glossy leaves floating outwards as she moved her hand, to reveal a cluster of tiny scarlet strawberries.' (p.34)

I have kept many of Lucy's letters to me written over the years and reading them now brings back so clearly the many happy visits that Margaret Clark and I made to Hemingford Grey. Immediately on arrival there was the tour of the garden, stopping at every rose bush to learn its history, to admire the colour and to savour the scent. Then to the table under the magnificent beech tree behind the house where there would be a bottle of very cold, very dry white wine — but no glasses, for the wine was to be drunk *from roses*. The first experience of this was both awe-inspiring and uncomfortable, for the wine tended to run down the hand and arm to the elbow, but it is amazing how accomplished you can become at anything with practice. Into the cool house for a delicious lunch and then the talk — about books and music, about people and gardens. Sometimes in the evening there was a candlelit concert in the Music Room; sometimes the planning of a party in London; always a lot of laughter. My memories of Lucy are happy ones.

I have been to the Manor only once since Lucy died and that was on the day of her funeral. The sun shone warmly, there were people spilling out of the house and into the garden. It was almost as if Lucy had never left — only not quite.

⌘

Toby H. Thompson

A Few Memories of Lucy M. Boston and the Old Manor, Hemingford Grey

Long before I met her, Lucy Boston was my heroine and my mentor. For the last twenty years of her life, I was fortunate to visit her at Hemingford Grey once or twice a year. During these visits to the Old Manor, Lucy favored me with a private glimpse into another age; she treated me to a two decade long fireside chat touching music and Catholicism, art and absurdities, ghosts, books, gardening, and love. While I should someday like to write out the great truths I feel she taught me, what I remember here with the deepest pleasure is the intimacy of Lucy's friendship and the small moments we shared. My brother was a Marshall Scholar at Emmanuel college in 1971 when I visited him on my first trip to England. At fifteen, I was greatly enjoying the misery I could inflict on my family at will. Finally, in exasperation, my brother turned on me. 'What is it you really want to do in England?' 'I want to meet Lucy Boston.' This was impossible, of course, and I knew it. 'Where does she live?' he asked. I had studied the Green Knowe books for years and had somehow decided that Lucy Boston must live in Huntingdonshire. 'Great.' My brother was relieved. 'That's the next county over. You can look her up in the phone book.' I knew that famous authors were unlisted, but gamely I went to the porter's lodge at Emmanuel and looked in the Cambridgeshire and Huntingdonshire phone book. Miraculously, there she was, L.M. Boston, the Old Manor, Hemingford Grey.

A call was made, a date was set, and soon after I found myself standing on Manor Road, my family delighted to leave me there, stranded, while they went to St Ives for the afternoon. I wandered around for a while, then hit on asking at the vicarage for directions to the Manor. The lady who answered the door, presumably the vicar's wife, cheerfully pointed me to a stile, over a field, and down a river path. This all sounded fine; I thanked her, clutching my copy of T*he Children of Green Knowe* and started off in search of the stile.

I was far too filled with teenaged dignity to admit that I didn't know what a stile could be, born and bred in the city as I was. I managed to find part of the moat and saw a sign that read 'Beware of Adders'. I didn't know adders from stiles but they sounded ominous enough to steer clear of the moat.

After much thrashing around, I broke out of the field and onto the river. In tableau, the first thing that greeted me was a woman surrounded by several men picnicking on the far side of the river. They were drinking champagne and laughing. The glasses clinked. 'I certainly hope that's not Mrs Boston,' I thought.

I hurried on down the river, glancing to my right at a Georgian house set in large grounds. 'It must be further on.' But the river walk ended and I retraced my steps. Three Chinese boys were playing in the dirt by the river path. 'Where,' I asked, now in desperation, 'is the Manor?' They pointed to the Georgian house behind me. But wait. Green Knowe, as everyone knows, is a Norman hall. This was clearly a Georgian house. Was I now stranded, thousands of miles from home, in the midst of stiles and adders, with no way to get home ever again?

At this dark hour, I caught a glimpse of a small woman in gardening clothes rising from a lawn chair. She approached the garden gate. 'You must be Toby,' she said, smiling.

After travail, mis-step and confusion, the sun broke through and I was home.

Years later, Lucy told me she didn't remember any first visit; it seemed quite natural that I had been visiting the Old Manor forever. But I never forgot that first day: the silence of a thousand years descending on that dining room, a small plane buzzing overhead, the quiet laughter of two people who seemed to have known each other all their lives.

Thereafter, each visit had its own theme, thanks to Lucy's wide and varied interests. Once it was church steeples. For some reason I had become obsessed by the church in the village and its legendary steeple at the bottom of the River Ouse. Lucy provided petrified timbers rescued from the tower, foolhardy bellringers, assorted village women decorating the church for a wedding (giving me the idea to marry there, which I did six months later) and Caroline Hemming teasing me about steeples without mercy.

At other times, the visit centered on the river, or fireworks, or the harpsichord. In the case of the latter, it might be Colin Tilney as a house guest with music laid on before supper, or a visit to Mary Potts in Cambridge for a private concert. More often or not, the theme centered on ghosts.

One evening, ten years or so ago, I went into the village for a newspaper. The woman at the counter asked me if I was staying at the Old Manor. When I said I was, she asked me if I was the one who had seen a white lady by the moat. I was properly impressed since this harrowing experience had occurred that afternoon. I don't know how the knowledge made it through the Hemingfords so quickly, but I am not one to underestimate the extra-sensory powers of English villages.

I also remember another occasion, the first night I spent in the guest bedroom at the Old Manor. Actually the night itself went by without incident. It was the following morning that I awoke to the sounds of people in my room. I knew that Lucy had constant visitors in to see the house but I was shocked to find them standing around my bed. They seemed to be speaking vague German and garbled French, apparently amused by the supine form buried under the covers. I roused myself and popped my head out, ready to say, 'Well, ha, ha, you caught me, didn't you?' There was nobody there.

Some years later, I told this story to Lucy's grandchildren and someone said, 'I think that happened to father the first night he slept here.'

Ghost story or not, it is one of my treasures of Green Knowe: the morning I was inspected by the Saxon and Norman sons of the house and, apparently, not found wanting.

That my poor wife was taken to Hemingford Grey

prior to our marriage to pass Lucy's inspection was entirely my idea. Fortunately, Lucy approved (I knew, of course, she would) and Margaret and I were married from the village church in 1988.

Lucy and Elisabeth Vellacott were guests of honour at our wedding party in Cambridge later that day. Somehow there was a mix up about the car and driver we hired and I will never forget standing in the parking lot at the Garden House Hotel in Cambridge waving Lucy and Elisabeth off home. The tires squealed, there was a cloud of exhaust as they were whisked away in a chauffered *sports car*. Lucy was game for anything, of course, as long as she could sit in front with the driver.

It is one of my favorite memories of Lucy; I keep it with the one of her sitting on the stairs at the Old Manor after a formidable cocktail party. She was up near her bedroom door, I was nearer the bathroom below, and she was regaling me with stories about the house. 'There are many secrets within its walls.' I shivered in delight; it was pure Gothic romance.

In Lucy's last letter to me she writes about her greatest love, her garden.

'I am still very lame, but adore the garden which Robin does for me. He and I visit every plant daily. I wish spring didn't rush past so quickly. Every day something goes over and something new comes.'

How could I better summarize the past twenty years' friendship with a woman I adored so fervently? The relentless rush of time, the bright spread of memories? It is all there. I can only say I am blessed indeed never to have left it.

⌘

Colin Tilney

In 1637, towards the end of a long life — though not nearly as long as Lucy's — Girolamo Frescobaldi, organist of St Peter's and improviser of genius, gathered together and published his final thoughts on two fashionable ground basses, the passacaglia and the chaconne. He called his selection *Cento Partite sopra Passacagli* — a hundred variations on the passacaglia. It is his longest and most passionate work, and Lucy loved it with passion, too. She never seemed to tire of it and always secretly hoped it would be included in the house concerts I played for her on the Robert Woffington harpsichord that she looked after for me at the Manor. *Cento Partite* has a wild energy that carries the listener helplessly from the first note to the last, and this driven ferocity enchanted Lucy and excited her.

She probably heard the piece the first time I played at Hemingford, shortly after my introduction to Lucy by Mary Potts, who taught me at Cambridge. That concert took place upstairs, in the glorious high, dim fortress where Lucy and Elisabeth Vellacott had played records to grateful airmen during the war. It is described in the last chapter of Lucy's first autobiography. We both afterwards regretted what we said or thought at the time. (Lucy in a letter: 'I have just re-read *Memory in a House* and came to you at the end. What a write-up of a face now lost in a beard. No wonder I complain.') And my ungracious failure to respond to the strange and lovely music room, inexcusable as it seems in print, had quite a sound reason in reality: there appeared — wrongly — to be no earthly way of getting the harpsichord up Lucy's desperately narrow and twisting staircase .... Lucy later agreed, reluctantly, to hold the concerts downstairs, where she cleared a shapely eighteenth-century sewing room and made a pleasant setting for listening to music. Frescobaldi's masterpiece was often on the programme.

Sitting among her guests, utterly still and absorbed ('I love having to listen hard'), Lucy was evidently translating the figures of music into shapes and colours, for in the winter of 1973 she finished and gave me a single-size patchwork quilt that was later exhibited, with others that she had made, at one of the King's Lynn Festivals. Its entry in the catalogue runs: 'Thirty variations on a Theme. Made for Colin Tilney as a small thank offering for playing Frescobaldi's 'Hundred Variations' in my house.' All the patches are of cotton; the theme (passacaglia bass) is a dotted brown, and the thirty rose-like clusters (variations) are worked in every colour from gallica red to tangerine yellow. As in the music, figures in one flower turn up, transformed, in the next, and the whole structure is rigorously controlled by a mind that took special delight in Bach fugues.

When I went to live in Canada in 1979, Lucy fretted

that there would be no more concerts on the Irish harpsichord, but she need not have worried: I almost certainly saw her more often after that than I had when I still lived in England. Besides, there were new and interesting things to discuss, particularly our now very different climates for growing roses. Ontario's winter is long and severe, but its summers are hot and intense. *Reine des Violettes* climbed to over fifteen feet for me and had to be buttressed with a specially built arch; for Lucy, who loved that rose more than any other, it remained puny and gave few blooms. (Lucy: 'Your letter about the miraculous year nearly reduced me to tears. So far only one rose is in flower here and three of my favourites have been dug up and burnt. Dieback takes a big branch every day. However, *Vesuve*, planted last year and cut down to the soil, produced last week a tiny push of growth and laid a bright flower on the ground. So that's two roses out!')

As Lucy approached the end of her life, I sensed that she was gradually laying her beloved garden to rest, knowing that she was becoming less and less able to do it justice. ('The sight of all the topiary waiting to be done by me, and only me terrifies me ... it has been the worst year ever, the record broken in every bad way. I have spent a small fortune trying to arrange that next year there shall be a grand show while I am still myself. I have done that for two years already, but the Powers that be have forbidden, it's not to be allowed.')

A chance postcard I sent her from Banff, in the Canadian Rockies, gave a revealing glimpse of her thoughts. (Lucy: 'Thank you, at long last, for the most wonderful view of mountains behind mountains and snow-covered crags in the sky. It is now stuck up on the door and gives me endless pleasure. You don't know what it is like never to leave your own garden, nice as it is, and to be reminded of what wonders there are in the world.') (Colin in a letter: 'It was not a good place to live, even for one week; too enclosed and the thrills too expected, though the air was wonderful. I think there are far distant parts of the north of Canada where nobody goes and where the mountain ranges hardly have names but go on and on for ever, one uninhabited valley after another and hundred-year-old trees eighteen inches high, because of the cold — that's perhaps the scenery I have at the back of my soul.')

That very ordinary tourist postcard continued to hold Lucy in its grip. ('Will you be going to your ghostly distant mountains? Look at them for me, it's a long time since I've had an eye stretch. I really know this view by now. But we had a deer at the dining room window at breakfast, so I felt liberated.') But her senses were becoming treacherous, and she lost a little of that amazing self-sufficiency. ('Caroline Hemming leaves me in two days, and after that I shall be alone here, I always have been, but used not to mind.') One thing consoled her: her hearing stayed as sharp as ever. ('I can do nothing but listen, which I do by the hour.') I recorded *Cento Partite* for an American company and sent her tapes of that, of Scarlatti sonatas and of Bach's 48 Preludes and Fugues, on harpischord and clavichord. ('Thank you all winter for the *Wohl Temperiert Clavier*.') And at a concert in London in 1988, at Fenton House in Hampstead, since I couldn't have Lucy herself in the audience, I prefaced Frescobaldi's 'Hundred Variations' with the beautiful sonnet Lucy had written about the piece some years earlier. Everyone in the room was almost unbearably moved by the music of the poetry. And Lucy herself was delighted. ('I find myself without words! Anything that links me with you, at the harpsichord, is so unexpected that I feel both insignificant and very proud. Thank you. It's enough to make me smile on my death bed! I think it was the first time you played in these Walls Upstairs.')

Passacaglia — by Lucy Boston

Though with long tension and with ambushed fall,
Sometimes to free us and sometimes entwine,
Music has bound our thoughts to its design
And our mis-beating hearts held close in thrall,
When the last note has travelled into space
We take deep breath and do not grieve at all,
But the bright coils of sound recall,
Of which the end is but the meeting place.
When the time comes that the last word is spoken
And you have turned away your face,
Farewell shall be the simple affirmation,
These walls were filled with joy and celebration
And courtesy and grace,
Though the long silence stretches out unbroken.

This then *was* love, Lucy - deep joy that you should be.

⌘

Lucy talks to her gardener. Painted by Elisabeth Vellacott, 1983/84

Ann Walshe

Lucy had one especially adverse effect on me: even when she was ninety she would stride past my kitchen window like a teenager and I swear that I aged at least five years every time I saw her.

She never accepted old age for herself; others yes. I am sure this is what kept her so remarkably alert, perceptive and creative up to the very end.

To illustrate this I would like to give one example. The BBC decided to do a full-length dramatization of her book *The Children of Green Knowe* in celebration of her ninetieth birthday. Lucy asked if she and her niece, Caroline, might come and watch it with us. At the end we were all discussing the production when Lucy came out with the remark 'The royalties will come in very useful for my Old Age!'

⌘

J.M. Walshe

My abiding memory of Lucy is, I suppose, of a sprightly ninety-year-old striding down the village street or digging in her garden with all the vigour and enthusiasm of a teenager. But the particular recollection which I would like to describe has a Thurberesque quality about it which almost merits the title of 'The night the bed fell on father'; after all it did occur at night and there was a bed involved, though in a minor capacity and it did not fall on anyone.

The event, I might almost call it an adventure, in question, took place towards the end of the 'striding down the village street' era. As Lucy had become rather less certain on her legs I had helped to persuade her to get a personal alarm; living alone in a twelfth-century house it seemed only prudent and Lucy agreed. The first call came shortly afterwards when Lucy got stuck in the bath, but she managed to extract herself before help arrived. The next alarm came some time later. It was in February at the height of a very cold spell. It was three o'clock in the morning when the telephone roused me from sleep. The voice at the other end informed me that they had had a signal from Mrs Boston at the Manor and could get no answer when they rang back — could I please go and see what the problem was. It was bitterly cold so while I rapidly donned as many clothes as I could, my mind ran over the possibilities. What would I find — a medical emergency, or perhaps a slip on the stairs and a broken leg or worse, a broken neck. At three o'clock in the morning there is no limit to the horrors one can dream up. Be that as it may I hurried down stairs, found a torch and a pair of gloves and set out down the village street and on to the footpath down the river bank to the wicket gate into the Manor grounds.

It was a beautiful night, a full moon, a savage frost sparkling on the trees, the moonbeams twinkling on the water and a light mist softening and making mysterious the view down towards Hemingford Abbots. Truly a sight never to be forgotten. However, it was with increasing apprehension that I climbed the gate, the easy way in, walked over to the shed where I knew the key was hidden, and let myself in. To my immense relief there was no crumpled body at the foot of the stairs or in the dining room. What would I find at the top of the stairs? Nothing. I knocked and entered Lucy's bedroom. Nothing. I turned on the light and looked around. Nothing. What had happened to Lucy? Had she been transfixed by hypothermia in the bathroom — the house was almost as cold inside as out. Lucy didn't believe in creature comforts. I called out and then I saw the bedclothes stir. An eye peeped out from under the sheets.

'Oh,' said Lucy, 'it's you. Why did you come?'

'Well, you rang your alarm.'

'Did I? Well anyway you're not a burglar. When I heard footsteps on the stairs I thought I was being robbed so I hid under the sheets!!'

'Why,' I said, 'didn't you answer the call service when they rang you back?'

'Oh well, I always take the receiver off at night, I have so many anonymous calls. 'Next time I come at night,' I said,'I will bring a bell and ring it, like a leper, so you will know who it is.'

I then did some brainwashing about the desirability of some heat in the bedroom which I think eventually bore fruit — she may have been used to the cold but I was not and if a rescue act were to become necessary it should be done in comfort. Anyway, all was well that ended well and I had a beautiful walk home — I really was grateful to Lucy for the call. Without it I should have missed the most beautiful view in the world.

⌘

Susan Walshe

One wonderful evening, twenty-four years ago, when I was twelve and Clare, my sister, was nine, Lucy invited us round for our very first dinner party. This in itself made the whole evening a very special one for us both and we were treated to lovely new dresses for such an important occasion.

By wonderful chance it was a brilliant moonlit evening, with stars twinkling brightly. The walk down the tow-path and the approach to Lucy's ancient house, beautifully silhouetted in the moonlight, lent to the feeling of a never-to-be-forgotten occasion.

After dinner by candlelight in the dining room, with the fire burning brightly, Lucy invited us all, our parents were with us, to gather round the fire. The moon seemed to be shining straight in on us, although my imagination was rampant and I would have believed anything. Lucy started to read to us. She read one of her very first Ghost Stories; at that time I think it had not been published. The atmosphere was complete magic, and still I get a tingle whenever I remember that wonderful evening, the like of which can never be repeated.

⌘

Nan Youngman

for Lucy's 80th Birthday

Lucy, her eyes as bright as any star
Upright she is, and let us praise her name.
Cuts her hair short. The sparkiest here by far.
Young Lucy puts us all, I swear, to shame.

And for her 95th Birthday

Lucy! Again the 10th December
Upright you stay. We praise your name
Cry 'Wine and Roses', friend, remember?
Young Lucy still puts me to shame.

⌘

Frank Collieson

From an obituary in *The Independent* 1 June 1990

Fools were suffered not at all by Lucy Boston, but to be a friend in her enchanted dining-room on a summer evening was such stuff as dreams are made on. The party would begin with goblets of champagne uncorked by male guests from the case provided each year by her devoted New York publisher, Margaret McElderry, who was married from the house. The door to the garden would be open and Lucy would proffer chocolate with her worn gardener's hands to the squirrels queueing on the terrace outside. Then dinner and wine, and the intoxication of Lucy's trenchant comments on fools and friends alike. You were there because you had proved youself responsive to the house and its magic. As the light failed, the dangling prisms on the Regency candelabra might unaccountably shimmer and tinkle however still the evening. If you remarked on this, Lucy might smile and say: 'We understand each other, the house and I — and each other's secrets.'

⌘

John Rowe Townsend

obituary in *The Guardian*, May 31st 1990

Lucy Boston seemed permanent: set to go on for ever in the ancient manor house known to readers all over the world as Green Knowe. Even in her nineties she could be found vigorously at work in the garden or leaning over her gate to chat to passers-by on the river bank who had the wit to admire her roses aloud. Everyone who knew her knew that when the day came she would die where she had lived; but it was hard to believe that the day would dare to come.

It was the house at Hemingford Grey, in Cambridgeshire - with its nine centuries of history and its atmosphere thick with the past, that inspired the books that made her famous. 'All my water,' she once said, 'is drawn from one well... I am obsessed by my house. It is in the highest degree a thing to be loved.' Her books in fact explored and re-explored the house, as an artist in any medium will explore and re-explore a theme that grips.

Lucy Boston came late to writing; her first book — an adult novel — was published when she was over

60. Though she wrote another adult novel, two books of autobiography, a play and poems, most of her work appeared on the children's lists. The children who read the early 'Green Knowe' books when they came out in the 1950s are middle aged now, but the books have stayed popular and been adapted for television.

In the first two, *The Children of Green Knowe*, and *The Chimneys of Green Knowe*, a small boy named Tolly goes to stay at the house with his grandmother, significantly named Mrs. Oldknow, and seems to meet children who lived there centuries ago. But there are subtle ambiguities here; does Tolly 'really' encounter these long-dead children in a time slip, or are they ghosts, or is it all an illusion, an effect of the house on his quickened imagination? I never dared ask Mrs. Boston, whom I knew in her later years as a softly-spoken but formidable old lady, for whom I had a deep admiration and affection, and even deeper awe. I think if one had asked her she would have smiled, declined to commit herself and thought privately 'What a stupid question!' We can hold more than one possibility in our minds at once.

There were four more Green Knowe books, of which the best was *A Stranger at Green Knowe*, published in 1961. The stranger is Hanno, a gorilla who has escaped from the zoo, and taken refuge in the Green Knowe garden. Hanno is shot in the end, but we're left in no doubt that it is better for him than going back to the zoo. The last of the six, which was also Lucy's last book, was *The Stones of Green Knowe* published in 1976, which went right back to the beginning, with a boy called Roger in 1120 watching the fine new manor house being built and travelling through time to meet Green

Knowe children from other periods and other books.

Lucy Boston was not, in my view, outstandingly good at constructing plots or portraying character. But she was a writer of distinction, and children who grew up on her work were the richer for it. Her sense of the past was subtle and haunting, and there was deep feeling in her work. She could be poetic and evocative, as when Tolly returns to Green Knowe and 'the wide and wandering garden was silky with daffodils.' She had a strong sense of the natural world, living and breathing, to be seen through the alert eye and felt through the fingertips. It was this awareness that she felt to be precious in children, that she wished to share with them, and that may have led her to write for them.

⌘

Margaret Clark

A Celebration for the Life and Work of Lucy Boston — 13th October, 1990

It was a day Lucy herself might have chosen: one of those autumnal afternoons 'that are like June come again but with a thrilling lightness in air and sky instead of languor.' The church of St Margaret at Hemingford Abbots was decorated for Harvest Festival; grapes hung from the lectern, apples shone red on grey stone windowsill. In the front pew sat Lucy's immediate family, eyes and profile almost heart-stopping in their likeness. The church, too, was filled with a thrilling lightness, the atmosphere charged with happiness and gratitude for a long life and talents well used.

The Archdeacon of Huntingdon opened the service by describing to the large congregation of family and friends Lucy's funeral in May, when one of her granddaughters had gone into the Manor garden early in the morning and picked from each of Lucy's beloved old rose-trees a flower to put on her coffin.

And now, the mourning over, the service that followed took the form of music and reminiscence. A

Cambridge friend, Howard Ferguson, recalled Lucy's delight in life and her unique hospitality. The composer, Ian Kellam, remembered how, as a young man, he had gloomily anticipated a weekend in the company of a seventy-year-old eccentric lady, only to find himself sleepily following Lucy round her garden in the early dawn, listening to her favourites among the chorus of sweet-throated birds. The music he had chosen to commemorate Lucy was Ping's Soliloquy from his *Green Knowe Suite* arranged for flute and piano.

Then, to speak of Lucy as Storyteller, came Peter Hollindale, whose essay 'The Darkening of the Green' had most appropriately pointed the topical importance of A *Stranger at Green Knowe*, appearing just before Lucy's first heart attack in March 1990.

At this invocation, as in the book, absolute silence followed, until the congregation let loose its emotion in the whole-hearted singing of a hymn which would have pleased Lucy's Evangelical forebears. There were even smiles at the third verse, 'Perverse and foolish oft I stray'd', as her autobiography of childhood and adolescence nearly a hundred years ago came to mind.

Now Colin Tilney, who had travelled from Canada especially for the occasion, spoke of how he had first introduced Lucy to the music of Frescobaldi, when she wrote of his playing the harpsichord in the Norman room at the Manor: 'After perhaps three and a half hours of mounting excitement ... he really took off in a roar of swarming notes, passionately interacting, reforming and flying off, so that my ears were incredulous of what they were hearing and the only possible reaction was blissful laughter.' (So it was now — as if Colin had called up her very spirit, speaking as he did of her thoughtfully listening with black eyebrows swooping in wonder, and reading aloud from her sonnet 'Passacaglia':

> When the last note has travelled into space
> We take deep breath and do not grieve at all,
> But the bright coils of sound recall,
> Of which the end is but the meeting place.

And so to the final reading by Peter Boston, whose introduction surprised even himself. He remembered sitting alone in the dining room of the Manor in 1937, when the restoration was just complete. He was absorbed in reading *War and Peace* when suddenly he was aware of a cold draught of air and the room was at once full of people — people in clothes of another age. He had no doubt of the truth of this experience, which he was convinced represented the welcome of those returning to the house as they had known it. Now he was equally sure that among their number would be a figure probably clothed in earth-coloured dungarees, happy to be in the place that, as she said when she first entered it, 'took me by the throat and filled me with a welcoming and headlong excitement'. Thus it was clear why Lucy's son had chosen to read this sonnet, written when she was in her eighties, as a farewell:

Walls

> These walls shall keep the joyful thought
> That, wondering in each deep recess
> In search of words, is now inwrought,
> Safe-kept in standing quietness.
> They shall entrap the spoken tone
> Lest its vibrations die in time and space,
> Here caught in crevices of stone

And anchored in its uttering-place.
And if in other time than this
That face should once again come home
That was intrinsic here
Ever re-moulded in the receiving air,
If he should brave the secret of this room
A ghost shall give a tangent kiss.

⌘